Celebration Hymnal

Edited by
KEVIN MAYHEW

MAYHEW - McCRIMMON
Great Wakering

First Published in Great Britain in 1976 by
MAYHEW - McCRIMMON LTD
Great Wakering
Essex

Compilation © Copyright 1976 by Mayhew-McCrimmon

ISBN 0 85597 094 4

Cover Design: Michael Green

Layout: Pam Hayden

Printer: Silver End Press, London & Essex

1

1. Abide with me,
      fast falls the eventide;
   the darkness deepens,
      Lord, with me abide!
   When other helpers fail,
      and comforts flee,
   help of the helpless,
      O abide with me.

2. Swift to its close
      ebbs out life's little day;
   earth's joys grow dim,
      its glories pass away;
   change and decay
      in all around I see;
   O thou who changest not,
      abide with me.

3. I need thy presence
      every passing hour;
   what but thy grace
      can foil the tempter's power?
   Who like thyself
      my guide and stay can be?
   Through cloud and sunshine,
      O abide with me.

4. I fear no foe with thee
      at hand to bless;
   ills have no weight,
      and tears no bitterness.
   Where is death's sting?
      Where, grave, thy victory?
   I triumph still,
      if thou abide with me.

5. Hold thou thy Cross before
      my closing eyes;
   shine through the gloom,
      and point me to the skies;
   heaven's morning breaks,
      and earth's vain shadows flee:
   in life, in death, O Lord,
      abide with me!

                    H. F. Lyte (1793-1847)

2

1. Accept, O Father, in thy love,
   these humble gifts of bread and
                                wine,
   that with ourselves we offer thee,
   returning gifts already thine.

2. Behold this host and chalice, Lord,
   to thee in heaven the gifts we raise;
   through them may we our homage
                                 pay,
   our adoration and our praise.

3. No earthly claim to grace is ours,
   save what thy sacrifice has won;
   grant then thy grace, fulfil our
                                needs,
   and may thy will in ours be done.

                          J. Clifford Evers

3

1. All creation, bless the Lord.
   Earth and heaven, bless the Lord.
   Spirits, powers, bless the Lord.
   Praise him for ever.
   Sun and moon, bless the Lord.
   Stars and planets, bless the Lord.
   Dews and showers, bless the Lord.
   Praise him for ever.

2. Winds and breezes, bless the Lord.
   Spring and Autumn, bless the Lord.
   Winter, Summer, bless the Lord.
   Praise him for ever.
   Fire and heat, bless the Lord.
   Frost and cold, bless the Lord.
   Ice and snow, bless the Lord.
   Praise him for ever.

3. Night and daytime, bless the Lord.
   Light and darkness, bless the Lord.
   Clouds and lightning, bless the Lord.
   Praise him for ever.
   All the earth, bless the Lord.
   Hills and mountains, bless the Lord.
   Trees and flowers, bless the Lord.
   Praise him for ever.

4. Springs and rivers, bless the Lord.
   Seas and oceans, bless the Lord.
   Whales and fishes, bless the Lord.
   Praise him for ever.
   Birds and insects, bless the Lord.
   Beasts and cattle, bless the Lord.
   Let all creatures bless the Lord.
   Praise him for ever.

5. Let God's people bless the Lord.
   Men and women, bless the Lord.
   All creation, bless the Lord.
   Praise him for ever.
   Let God's people bless the Lord.
   Men and women, bless the Lord.
   All creation, bless the Lord.
   Praise him for ever.

Hayward Osborne

4

1. All creatures of our God and King,
   lift up your voice and with us sing
   alleluia, alleluia!
   Thou burning sun with golden
                              beam,
   thou silver moon with softer gleam:

   O praise him, O praise him,
   alleluia, alleluia, alleluia.

2. Thou rushing wind that art so
                              strong,
   ye clouds that sail in heaven along,
   O praise him, alleluia!
   Thou rising morn, in praise rejoice,
   ye lights of evening, find a voice:

3. Thou flowing water, pure and clear,
   make music for thy Lord to hear,
   alleluia, alleluia!
   Thou fire so masterful and bright,
   that givest man both warmth and
                              light:

4. Dear mother earth, who day by day
   unfoldest blessings on our way,
   O praise him, alleluia!
   The flowers and fruits that in thee
                              grow
   let them his glory also show.

5. And all ye men of tender heart,
   forgiving others, take your part,
   O sing ye, alleluia!
   Ye who long pain and sorrow bear,
   praise God and on him cast your
                              care:

6. And thou, most kind and gentle
                              death,
   waiting to hush our latest breath,
   O praise him, alleluia!
   Thou leadest home the child of
                              God,
   and Christ our Lord the way hath
                              trod:

7. Let all things their Creator bless,
   and worship him in humbleness,
   O praise him, alleluia!
   Praise, praise the Father, praise the
                              Son,
   and praise the Spirit, Three in One.

W. H. Draper (1855-1933)
Based on the Cantico di Frate Sole of
St. Francis of Assisi (1182-1226)

5

1. Alleluia, alleluia,
   alleluia, alleluia,
   alleluia, alleluia,
   alleluia, alleluia.

2. Jesus is Lord, . . .

3. And I love him, . . .

4. Christ is risen, . . .

Traditional

6

Alleluia, alleluia!
I will praise the Father
   for all of my life,
I will sing to my God
   as long as I live,
alleluia, alleluia, alleluia!

1. Do not place all your trust
      in the power of man:
   he cannot save.
   His schemes will all perish
      when he yields up his breath
   at the end of his day.

2. But so happy the man
      who will trust in his God:
   he will find help.
   For he is the maker
      of the heavens and earth
   and of all that these hold.

3. All the searchers for justice,
      for freedom, for love,
   he will fulfil.
   The widow, the orphan,
      and the blind and the lame
   in his love are restored.

Based on Psalm 146
by Michael Cockett

7

1. Alleluia, sing to Jesus,
   his the sceptre, his the throne,
   alleluia, his the triumph,
   his the victory alone:
   hark the songs of peaceful Sion
   thunder like a mighty flood:
   Jesus, out of every nation,
   hath redeemed us by his blood.

2. Alleluia, not as orphans
   are we left in sorrow now;
   alleluia, he is near us,
   faith believes, nor questions how;
   though the cloud from sight received
                                    him
   when the forty days were o'er,
   shall our hearts forget his promise,
   'I am with you evermore'?

3. Alleluia, Bread of Angels,
   thou on earth our food, our stay;
   alleluia, here the sinful
   flee to thee from day to day;
   intercessor, friend of sinners,
   earth's Redeemer, plead for me,
   where the songs of all the sinless
   sweep across the crystal sea.

4. Alleluia, King eternal
   thee the Lord of lords we own;
   alleluia, born of Mary,
   earth thy footstool, heaven thy
                                 throne;
   thou within the veil hast entered,
   robed in flesh, our great High Priest;
   thou on earth both priest and
                                 victim
   in the Eucharistic Feast.

W. Chatterton Dix (1837-98)

8

All glory, laud and honour,
to thee, Redeemer King,
to whom the lips of children
made sweet hosannas ring.

1. Thou art the King of Israel,
   thou David's royal Son,
   who in the Lord's name comest,
   the King and blessed one.

2. The company of angels
   are praising thee on high,
   and mortal men and all things
   created make reply.

3. The people of the Hebrews
   with palms before thee went:
   our praise and prayer and anthems
   before thee we present.

4. To thee before thy passion
   they sang their hymns of praise;
   to thee now high exalted
   our melody we raise.

5. Thou didst accept their praises,
   accept the prayers we bring,
   who in all good delightest,
   thou good and gracious king.

St Theodulph of Orleans (821),
tr. J. M. Neale

9

1. All hail the power of Jesus' name;
   let angels prostrate fall;
   bring forth the royal diadem
   To crown him, crown him,
   crown him,
   crown him Lord of all.

2. Crown him, ye martyrs of your
                              God,
   who from his altar call;
   praise him whose way of pain ye
                              trod,
   and crown him Lord of all.

3. Ye prophets who our freedom won,
   ye searchers, great and small,
   by whom the work of truth is done,
   now crown him Lord of all.

4. Sinners, whose love can ne'er forget
   the wormwood and the gall,
   go spread your trophies at his feet,
   and crown him Lord of all.

5. Bless him, each poor oppresséd race
   that Christ did upward call;
   his hand in each achievement trace,
   and crown him Lord of all.

6. Let every tribe and every tongue
   to him their hearts enthral:
   lift high the universal song,
   and crown him Lord of all.

   E. Perronet (1762-92), and others

10

1. All people that on earth do dwell,
   sing to the Lord with cheerful voice;
   him serve with fear, his praise forth
                                     tell,
   come ye before him and rejoice.

2. The Lord, ye know, is God indeed,
   without our aid he did us make;
   we are his folk, he doth us feed
   and for his sheep he doth us take.

3. O enter then his gates with praise,
   approach with joy his courts unto;
   praise, laud, and bless his name
                              always,
   for it is seemly so to do.

4. For why? the Lord our God is good:
   his mercy is for ever sure;
   his truth at all times firmly stood,
   and shall from age to age endure.

5. To Father, Son and Holy Ghost,
   the God whom heaven and earth
                              adore,
   from men and from the angel-host
   be praise and glory evermore.

   William Kethe, Day's Psalter (1560)

11

1. All that I am, all that I do,
   all that I'll ever have,
      I offer now to you.
   Take and sanctify these gifts
   for your honour, Lord.
   Knowing that I love and serve you
   is enough reward.
   All that I am, all that I do,
   all that I'll ever have
      I offer now to you.

2. All that I dream, ail that I pray,
   all that I'll ever make,
      I give to you today.
   Take and sanctify these gifts
   for your honour, Lord.
   Knowing that I love and serve you
   is enough reward.
   All that I am, all that I do,
   all that I'll ever have
      I offer now to you.

   Sebastian Temple

12

All the nations of the earth,
praise the Lord who brings to birth
the greatest star, the smallest flower.
Alleluia.

1. Let the heavens praise the Lord.
   Alleluia.
   Moon and stars, praise the Lord.
   Alleluia.

2. Snow capped mountains,
      praise the Lord.
   Alleluia.
   Rolling hills, praise the Lord.
   Alleluia.

3. Deep sea water, praise the Lord.
   Alleluia.
   Gentle rain, praise the Lord.
   Alleluia.

4. Roaring lion, praise the Lord.
   Alleluia.
   Singing birds, praise the Lord.
   Alleluia.

5. Kings and princes, praise the Lord.
   Alleluia.
   Young and old, praise the Lord.
   Alleluia.

Michael Cockett

13

1. All things bright and beautiful,
   all creatures great and small,
   all things wise and wonderful,
   the Lord God made them all.

2. Each little flower that opens,
   each little bird that sings,
   he made their glowing colours,
   he made their tiny wings.

3. The purple-headed mountain,
   the river running by,
   the sunset and the morning,
   that brightens up the sky.

4. The cold wind in the winter,
   the pleasant summer sun,
   the ripe fruits in the garden,
   he made them every one.

5. The tall trees in the greenwood,
   the meadows for our play,
   the rushes by the water,
   to gather every day.

6. He gave us eyes to see them,
   and lips that we may tell
   how great is God Almighty,
   who has made all things well.

C. F. Alexander (1818-95)

14

1. All this world belongs to Jesus,
   ev'rything is his by right;
   all on the land, all in the sea;
   ev'rything is his by right.

2. Shining stars in all their beauty
   are outnumbered by his gifts.
   Sand on the shore, stars in the sky,
   are outnumbered by his gifts.

3. Ev'ry foot that starts a-dancing
   taps a rhythm full of hope;
   full of his joy, full of his hope,
   taps a rhythm full of hope.

4. All that's good reflects his goodness;
   may it lead us back to him.
   All that is good, all that is true,
   may it lead us back to him.

5. So give thanks for what he's given;
   touch and taste, and feet to dance;
   eyes for the lights, ears for the sound,
   for the wonders of our Lord.

Willard F. Jabusch

15

1. All ye who seek a comfort sure
   in trouble and distress,
   whatever sorrow vex the mind,
   or guilt the soul oppress:

2. Jesus, who gave himself for you
   upon the cross to die,
   opens to you his sacred heart;
   oh, to that heart draw nigh.

3. Ye hear how kindly he invites;
   ye hear his words so blest:
   'All ye that labour come to me,
   and I will give you rest.'

4. Jesus, thou joy of saints on high,
   thou hope of sinners here,
   attracted by those loving words
   to thee I lift my prayer.

5. Wash thou my wounds in that dear
                                 blood,
   which forth from thee doth flow;
   new grace, new hope inspire, a new
   and better heart bestow.

                    18th c., tr. Edward Caswall

16

*All you peoples, clap your hands
and shout for joy.
The Lord has made all mankind one,
so raise your voices high.*

1. All creation shows
   the glory of the Lord.
   The earth proclaims his handiwork,
   the sky cries out his word.
   Night and day sing out
   the glories all about,
   so praise the Lord with shouts of
                                  joy.

2. The king of all the earth
   has made his message known,
   that we should offer him ourselves
   and ev'rything we own.
   We do this by the way
   we live through ev'ry day.
   So live each day in peace and joy.

3. The kingdom of the Lord
   was made for all the good;
   those who want to live in peace
   and brotherhood.
   So with our fellow man
   let's all join hand to hand
   and praise the Lord with shouts of
                                  joy.

4. Let ev'ry man alive
   remember your command,
   that ev'ry day in ev'ry way
   we love our fellow man.
   If this command is done,
   the vict'ry will be won,
   and we'll live in peace and joy.

                                  Ray Repp

17

1. Almighty Father, Lord most high,
   who madest all, who fillest all,
   thy name we praise and magnify,
   for all our needs on thee we call.

2. We offer to thee of thine own,
   ourselves and all that we can bring,
   in bread and cup before thee shown,
   our universal offering.

3. All that we have we bring to thee,
   yet all is naught when all is done,
   save that in it thy love can see
   the sacrifice of thy dear Son.

4. By this command in bread and cup,
   his body and his blood we plead;
   what on the cross he offer'd up
   is here our sacrifice indeed.

5. For all thy gifts of life and grace,
   here we thy servants humbly pray
   that thou would'st look upon the
                                  face
   of thine anointed Son today.

            *Vincent Stuckley Stratton Coles
                             (1845-1929)*

18

1. Almighty Father, take this bread
   thy people offer thee;
   where sins divide us, take instead
   one fold and family.

2. The wine we offer soon will be
   Christ's blood, redemption's price;
   receive it, Holy Trinity,
   this holy sacrifice.

3. O God, by angels' choirs adored,
   thy name be praised on earth;
   on all men be that peace outpoured
   once promised at his birth.

   Anonymous

19

1. Amazing grace! How sweet the
                              sound
   that saved a wretch like me.
   I once was lost but now I'm found,
   was blind, but now I see.

2. 'Twas grace that taught my heart to
                               fear,
   and grace my fears relieved.
   How precious did that grace appear
   the hour I first believed.

3. Through many dangers, toils and
                               snares
   I have already come.
   'Tis grace hath brought me safe thus
                               far,
   and grace will lead me home.

4. The Lord has promised good to me;
   his word my hope secures.
   He will my shield and portion be
   as long as life endures.

   John Newton

20

1. And did those feet in ancient time
   walk upon England's mountains
                              green?
   And was the holy Lamb of God
   on England's pleasant pastures
                              seen?
   And did the countenance divine
   shine forth upon our clouded hills?
   And was Jerusalem buildéd here
   among those dark Satanic mills?

2. Bring me my bow of burning gold!
   Bring me my arrows of desire!
   Bring me my spear! O clouds,
                              unfold!
   Bring me my chariot of fire!
   I will not cease from mental fight,
   nor shall my sword sleep in my
                              hand,
   till we have built Jerusalem
   in England's green and pleasant
                              land.

   William Blake (1757-1827)

21

1. Angels we have heard in heaven
   sweetly singing o'er our plains,
   and the mountain-tops in answer
   echoing their joyous strains.

   Gloria in excelsis Deo.

2. Shepherds, why this exultation?
   Why your rapturous strain prolong?
   Tell us of the gladsome tidings,
   which inspire your joyous song.

3. Come to Bethlehem, and see him
   o'er whose birth the angels sing,
   come, adore, devoutly kneeling,
   Christ the Lord, the new-born king.

4. See him in a manger lying
   whom the choir of angels praise!
   Mary, Joseph, come to aid us
   while our hearts in love we raise.

   James Chadwick (1813-82)

22

1. Angels we have heard on high
sweetly singing o'er our plains,
and the mountains in reply
echo still their joyous strains.

Gloria in excelsis Deo.

2. Shepherds, why this jubilee?
Why your rapturous strain prolong?
Say, what may your tidings be,
which inspire your heavenly song.

3. Come to Bethlehem and see
him whose birth the angels sing:
come, adore on bended knee
the infant Christ, the new-born
King.

4. See within a manger laid,
Jesus, Lord of heaven and earth!
Mary, Joseph, lend your aid
to celebrate our Saviour's birth.

James Chadwick (1813-82)

23

Ask, and you will receive.
Seek, and you will find.
Knock, and the door will be opened
for the love of the Lord has no end.

1. Is there any man here,
when his son asks for bread,
would turn him away
with a stone instead?
Is there any man here,
when his son asks for meat,
would then give him
a poisonous snake to eat?

2. So then how could your Father
in heaven above,
who knows so much more
of the ways of love,
so then how could your Father
refuse what is good,
when you ask in the name
of the Son he loves?

3. So whatever you ask
you will always receive,
whatever you seek
you will always find.
For my Father will give
to all those who believe
in the Spirit of love
that will never end.

Michael Cockett

24

1. As with gladness men of old,
did the guiding star behold,
as with joy they hailed its light,
leading onward, beaming bright,
so, most gracious God, may we
evermore be led to thee.

2. As with joyful steps they sped,
to that lowly manger-bed,
there to bend the knee before
him whom heaven and earth adore,
so may we with willing feet
ever seek thy mercy-seat.

3. As they offered gifts most rare,
at that manger rude and bare,
so may we with holy joy,
pure, and free from sin's alloy,
all our costliest treasures bring,
Christ, to thee our heavenly King.

4. Holy Jesu, every day
keep us in the narrow way;
and, when earthly things are past,
bring our ransomed souls at last
where they need no star to guide,
where no clouds thy glory hide.

5. In the heavenly country bright
need they no created light,
thou its Light, its Joy, its Crown,
thou its Sun which goes not down;
there for ever may we sing
alleluias to our King.

William Chatterton Dix (1837-98)

25

1. Attend and keep this happy fast
   I preach to you this day.
   Is this the fast that pleases me
   that takes your joy away?
   Do I delight in sorrow's dress,
   says God, who reigns above,
   the hanging head, the dismal look,
   will they attract my love?

2. But is this not the fast I choose,
   that shares the heavy load;
   that seeks to bring the poor man in
   who's weary of the road;
   that gives the hungry bread to eat,
   to strangers gives a home;
   that does not let you hide your face
   from your own flesh and bone?

3. Then like the dawn your light will
                                    break,
   to life you will be raised.
   And men will praise the Lord for
                                    you;
   be happy in your days.
   The glory of the Lord will shine,
   and in your steps his grace.
   And when you call he'll answer you;
   he will not hide his face.

   Roger Ruston, after Isaiah 58: 5-9

26

1. At the cross her station keeping,
   stood the mournful mother
                           weeping,
   close to Jesus to the last;

2. Through her heart, his sorrow
                           sharing,
   all his bitter anguish bearing,
   now at length the sword has pass'd.

3. Oh, how sad and sore distress'd
   was that mother highly blest,
   of the sole-begotten One.

4. Christ above in torment hangs;
   she beneath beholds the pangs
   of her dying glorious Son.

5. Is there one who would not weep,
   whelm'd in miseries so deep,
   Christ's dear mother to behold?

6. Can the human heart refrain
   from partaking in her pain,
   in that mother's pain untold?

7. Bruised, derided, cursed, defiled,
   she beheld her tender child,
   all with bloody scourges rent;

8. For the sins of his own nation,
   saw him hang in desolation,
   till his spirit forth he sent.

9. O thou mother! fount of love!
   Touch my spirit from above,
   make my heart with thine accord:

10. Make me feel as thou hast felt;
    make my soul to glow and melt
    with the love of Christ my Lord.

11. Holy Mother, pierce me through,
    in my heart each wound renew
    of my Saviour crucified.

12. Let me share with thee his pain
    who for all my sins was slain,
    who for me in torments died.

13. Let me mingle tears with thee,
    mourning him who mourn'd for me,
    all the days that I may live:

14. By the cross with thee to stay,
    there with thee to weep and pray,
    is all I ask of thee to give.

15. Virgin of all virgins best,
    listen to my fond request:
    let me share thy grief divine;

16. Let me, to my latest breath,
    in my body bear the death
    of that dying son of thine.

17. Wounded with his every wound,
    steep my soul till it hath swoon'd
    in his very blood away.

18. Be to me, O Virgin, nigh,
    lest in flames I burn and die,
    in his awful judgement day.

19. Christ, when thou shalt call me hence,
   be thy mother my defence,
   be thy cross my victory.

20. While my body here decays,
   may my soul thy goodness praise,
   safe in paradise with thee.

Ascribed to Jacopone da Todi (d. 1306),
tr. E. Caswall

27

1. At the Lamb's high feast we sing
   praise to our victorious king,
   who hath washed us in the tide
   flowing from his piercéd side.
   Praise we him whose love divine
   gives the guests his blood for wine,
   gives his body for the feast,
   love the victim, love the priest.

2. Where the paschal blood is poured,
   Death's dark angel sheathes his
                                   sword;
   Israel's hosts triumphant go
   through the wave that drowns the
                                   foe.
   Christ the Lamb, whose blood was
                                   shed.
   Paschal victim, paschal bread;
   with sincerity and love
   eat we manna from above.

3. Mighty victim from the sky,
   powers of hell beneath thee lie;
   death is conquered in the fight;
   thou hast brought us life and light,
   now thy banner thou dost wave;
   vanquished Satan and the grave;
   angels join his praise to tell —
   see o'erthrown the prince of hell.

4. Paschal triumph, paschal joy,
   only sin can this destroy;
   from the death of sin set free
   souls re-born, dear Lord, in thee.
   Hymns of glory, songs of praise,
   Father, unto thee we raise.
   Risen Lord, all praise to thee,
   ever with the Spirit be.

7th c., tr. Robert Campbell

28

1. At the name of Jesus
   every knee shall bow,
   every tongue confess him
   King of glory now;
   'tis the Father's pleasure
   we should call him Lord,
   who from the beginning,
   was the mighty Word.

2. At his voice creation
   sprang at once to sight,
   all the Angel faces,
   all the hosts of light,
   thrones and dominations,
   stars upon their way,
   all the heavenly orders,
   in their great array.

3. Humbled for a season,
   to receive a name
   from the lips of sinners
   unto whom he came,
   faithfully he bore it
   spotless to the last,
   brought it back victorious
   when from death he passed:

4. Bore it up triumphant
   with its human light
   through all ranks of creatures,
   to the central height,
   to the throne of Godhead,
   to the Father's breast,
   filled it with the glory
   of that perfect rest.

5. Name him, brothers, name him,
   with love as strong as death;
   but with awe and wonder,
   and with bated breath.
   He is God the Saviour,
   he is Christ the Lord,
   ever to be worshipped,
   trusted, and adored.

6. In your hearts enthrone him;
there let him subdue
all that is not holy,
all that is not true;
crown him as your captain;
in temptation's hour
let his will enfold you
in its light and power.

7. Brothers, this Lord Jesus
shall return again,
with his Father's glory,
with his angel train,
for all wreaths of empire
meet upon his brow,
and our hearts confess him
King of glory now.

Caroline Maria Noel (1817-77)

29

1. Ave Maria, O Maiden, O Mother,
fondly thy children are calling on
thee;
thine are the graces unclaimed by
another,
sinless and beautiful Star of the sea.

Mater amabilis, ora pro nobis,
pray for thy children who call upon
thee;
Ave sanctissima, Ave purissima
sinless and beautiful Star of the sea.

2. Ave Maria, the night shades are
falling,
softly, our voices arise unto thee;
earth's lonely exiles for succour are
calling,
sinless and beautiful Star of the sea.

3. Ave Maria, thy children are
kneeling,
words of endearment are murmured
to thee;
softly thy spirit upon us is stealing,
sinless and beautiful Star of the sea.

'Sister M.'

30

1. Away in a manger,
no crib for a bed,
the little Lord Jesus
laid down his sweet head,
the stars in the bright sky
looked down where he lay,
the little Lord Jesus
asleep on the hay.

2. The cattle are lowing,
the baby awakes,
but little Lord Jesus
no crying he makes.
I love thee, Lord Jesus!
Look down from the sky,
and stay by my side
until morning is nigh.

3. Be near me, Lord Jesus;
I ask thee to stay
close by me for ever,
and love me, I pray.
Bless all the dear children
in thy tender care,
and fit us for heaven,
to live with thee there.

J. Kirkpatrick

31

1. Battle is o'er,
hell's armies flee:
raise we the cry of victory
with abounding joy resounding,
alleluia.

2. Christ who endured
the shameful tree,
o'er death triumphant welcome we,
our adoring praise outpouring,
alleluia.

3. On the third morn
from death rose he,
clothed with what light in heaven
shall be,
our unswerving faith deserving,
alleluia.

4. Hell's gloomy gates
   yield up their key,
   paradise door thrown wide we see;
   never-tiring be our choiring,
   alleluia.

5. Lord, by the stripes
   men laid on the,
   grant us to live from death set free,
   this our greeting still repeating,
   alleluia.

   Simphonia Sirenum (1695)
   tr. Ronald Arbuthnott Knox

32

1. Be still, and know I am with you,
   be still, I am the Lord.
   I will not leave you orphans.
   I leave with you my world.
   Be one.

2. You fear the light may be fading,
   you fear to lose your way.
   Be still, and know I am near you.
   I'll lead you to the day
   and the sun.

3. Be glad the day you have sorrow,
   be glad, for then you live.
   The stars shine only in darkness,
   and in your need I give
   my peace.

   Sister Jude

33

1. Be still and know that I am God,
   be still and know that I am God,
   be still and know that I am God.

2. I am the Lord that healeth thee,
   I am the Lord that healeth thee,
   I am the Lord that healeth thee.

3. In thee, O Lord, I put my trust,
   in thee, O Lord, I put my trust,
   in thee, O Lord, I put my trust.

   Anonymous

34

1. Bethlehem! of noblest cities
   none can once with thee compare;
   thou alone the Lord from heaven
   didst for us incarnate bear.

2. Fairer than the sun at morning
   was the star that told his birth,
   to the lands their God announcing,
   hid beneath a form of earth.

3. By its lambent beauty guided,
   see the eastern kings appear;
   see them bend, their gifts to offer —
   gifts of incense, gold and myrrh.

4. Solemn things of mystic meaning!
   Incense doth the God disclose;
   gold a royal child proclaimeth;
   Myrrh a future tomb foreshows.

5. Holy Jesu, in they brightness
   to the gentile world display'd,
   with the Father and the Spirit,
   endless praise to thee be paid.

   Aurelius Prudentius (348-413),
   tr. E. Caswall

35

1. Be thou my vision,
      O Lord of my heart,
   naught be all else to me
      save that thou art;
   thou my best thought
      in the day and night,
   waking or sleeping,
      thy presence my light.

2. Be thou my wisdom,
      be thou my true word,
   I ever with thee and
      thou with me, Lord;
   thou my great Father,
      and I thy true son;
   thou in me dwelling,
      and I with thee one.

3. Be thou my breast-plate,
    my sword for the fight,
    be thou my armour,
    and be thou my might,
    thou my soul's shelter,
    and thou my high tower,
    raise thou me heavenward,
    O Power of my power.

4. Riches I heed not,
    nor man's empty praise,
    thou mine inheritance
    through all my days;
    thou, and thou only,
    the first in my heart,
    high King of heaven,
    my treasure thou art!

5. High King of heaven
    when battle is done,
    grant heaven's joy to me,
    O bright heaven's sun;
    Christ of my own heart,
    whatever befall,
    still be my vision,
    O Ruler of all.

Irish (8th C.), tr. Mary Byrne,
versified by Eleanor Hull

36

1. Blest are the pure in heart,
    for they shall see our God;
    the secret of the Lord is theirs,
    their soul is Christ's abode.

2. The Lord who left the heavens
    our life and peace to bring,
    to dwell in lowliness with men,
    their pattern and their king.

3. Still to the lowly soul
    he doth himself impart
    and for his dwelling and his throne
    chooseth the pure in heart.

4. Lord, we thy presence seek;
    may ours this blessing be:
    give us a pure and lowly heart,
    a temple meet for thee.

Verses 1 and 3 by John Keble
(1792-1866) verses 2 and 4 from
W. J. Hall's Psalms and Hymns (1836)

37

1. Breathe on me, Breath of God,
    fill me with life anew,
    that I may love what thou dost love,
    and do what thou wouldst do.

2. Breathe on me, Breath of God,
    until my heart is pure:
    until with thee I have one will
    to do and to endure.

3. Breathe on me, Breath of God,
    till I am wholly thine,
    until this earthly part of me
    glows with thy fire divine.

4. Breathe on me, Breath of God,
    so shall I never die,
    but live with thee the perfect life
    of thine Eternity.

Edwin Hatch (1835-89)

38

1. Bring, all ye dear-bought nations,
                                bring,
    your richest praises to your king,
                    alleluia, alleluia,
    that spotless Lamb, who more than
                                    due,
    paid for his sheep, and those sheep
                                    you,
    Alleluia.

2. That guiltless Son, who bought
                        your peace,
    and made his Father's anger cease,
    then, life and death together fought,
    each to a strange extreme were
                            brought.

3. Life died, but soon revived again,
    and even death by it was slain.
    Say, happy Magdalen, oh, say,
    what didst thou see there by the
                            way?

4. "I saw the tomb of my dear Lord,
I saw himself, and him adored,
I saw the napkin and the sheet,
that bound his head and wrapt his
feet."

5. "I heard the angels witness bear,
Jesus is ris'n; he is not here;
go, tell his followers they shall see,
thine and their hope in Galilee."

6. We, Lord, with faithful hearts and
voice,
on this thy rising day rejoice.
O thou, whose power o'ercame the
grave,
by grace and love us sinners save.

Wipo (11th C.),
tr. Walter Kirkham Blount

39

1. Bring flowers of the rarest,
bring blossoms the fairest,
from garden and woodland
and hillside and dale;
our full hearts are swelling,
our glad voices telling
the praise of the loveliest
flower of the vale.

O Mary we crown thee
with blossoms today.
Queen of the Angels
and Queen of the May.
O Mary we crown thee
with blossoms today,
Queen of the Angels
and Queen of the May.

2. Their lady they name thee,
their mistress proclaim thee.
Oh, grant that thy children
on earth be as true,
as long as the bowers
are radiant with flowers
as long as the azure shall
keep its bright hue.

3. Sing gaily in chorus,
the bright angels o'er us
re-echo the strains we
begin upon earth;
their harps are repeating
the notes of our greeting,
for Mary herself is the
cause of our mirth.

Anonymous

40

1. By the blood that flow'd from thee
in thy grievous agony;
by the traitor's guileless kiss,
filling up thy bitterness;

Jesus, saviour, hear our cry;
thou wert suff'ring once as we:
now enthron'd in majesty
countless angels sing to thee.

2. By the cords that, round thee cast,
bound thee to the pillar fast,
by the scourge so meekly borne,
by the purple robe of scorn.

3. By the thorns that crown'd thy
head,
by the sceptre of a reed;
by thy foes on bending knee,
mocking at thy royalty.

4. By the people's cruel jeers;
by the holy women's tears;
by thy footsteps, faint and slow,
weigh'd beneath thy cross of woe;

5. By thy weeping mother's woe;
by the sword that pierced her
through,
when in anguish standing by,
on the cross she saw thee die.

Frederick William Faber (1814-63)

41

1. Christ be beside me,
   Christ be before me,
   Christ be behind me,
   King of my heart.
   Christ be within me,
   Christ be below me,
   Christ be above me,
   never to part.

2. Christ on my right hand,
   Christ on my left hand,
   Christ all around me,
   shield in the strife.
   Christ in my sleeping,
   Christ in my sitting,
   Christ in my rising,
   light of my life.

3. Christ be in all hearts
   thinking about me,
   Christ be in all tongues
   telling of me.
   Christ be the vision
   in eyes that see me,
   in ears that hear me,
   Christ ever be.

Adapted from 'St. Patrick's Breastplate'
by James Quinn

42

1. Christ is King of earth and heaven!
   Let his subjects all proclaim
   in the splendour of his temple
   honour to his holy name.

2. Christ is King! No soul created
   can refuse to bend the knee
   to the God made man who reigneth
   as 'twas promised, from the tree.

3. Christ is King! Let humble sorrow
   for our past neglect atone,
   for the lack of faithful service
   to the Master whom we own.

4. Christ is King! Let joy and gladness
   greet him; let his courts resound
   with the praise of faithful subjects
   to his love in honour bound.

5. Christ is King! In health and
                sickness,
   till we breathe our latest breath,
   till we greet in highest heaven,
   Christ the victor over death.

Ivor J. E. Daniel (1883-1967)

43

Christ is our king,
*   let the whole world rejoice!*
May all the nations
*   sing out with one voice!*
Light of the world,
*   you have helped us to see*
that all men are brothers
*   and all men one day will be free.*

1. He came to open
      the eyes of the blind,
   letting the sunlight pour
      into their minds.
   Vision is waiting for
      those who have hope.
   He is the light of the world.

2. He came to speak
      tender words to the poor,
   he is the gateway and
      he is the door.
   Riches are waiting for all
      those who hope.
   He is the light of the world.

3. He came to open
      the doors of the gaol,
   he came to help the
      downtrodden and frail.
   Freedom is waiting for
      all those who hope.
   He is the light of the world.

4. He came to open
      the lips of the mute,
   letting them speak out
      with courage and truth.
   His words are uttered by
      all those who hope.
   He is the light of the world.

5. He came to heal all
    the crippled and lame,
   sickness took flight at the
      sound of his name.
   Vigour is waiting for
      all those who hope.
   He is the light of the world.

6. He came to love
      every man on this earth
   and through his Spirit he
      promised rebirth.
   New life is waiting for
      all those who hope.
   He is the light of the world.

Estelle White

44

1. Christ the Lord is risen today!
   Christians, haste your vows to pay,
   offer ye your praises meet
   at the paschal victim's feet;
   for the sheep the Lamb hath bled,
   sinless in the sinner's stead.
   Christ the Lord is ris'n on high;
   now he lives, no more to die.

2. Christ, the victim undefiled,
   man to God hath reconciled
   when in strange and awful strife
   met together death and life;
   Christians, on this happy day
   haste with joy your vows to pay.
   Christ the Lord is ris'n on high;
   Now he lives, no more to die.

3. Say, O wond'ring Mary, say,
   what thou sawest on thy way.
   "I beheld, where Christ had lain,
   empty tomb and angels twain,
   I beheld the glory bright
   of the rising Lord of light;
   Christ my hope is ris'n again;
   now he lives, and lives to reign."

4. Christ, who once for sinners bled,
   now the first-born from the dead,
   throned in endless might and
                              power,
   lives and reigns for evermore.
   Hail, eternal hope on high!
   Hail, thou king of victory!
   Hail, thou Prince of life adored!
   Help and save us, gracious Lord.

Wipo 11th c., tr. Jane Elizabeth Leeson

45

1. Colours of day
      dawn into the mind,
   the sun has come up,
      the night is behind.
   Go down in the city,
      into the street,
   and let's give the message
      to the people we meet.

   So light up the fire
      and let the flame burn,
   open the door, let Jesus return.
   Take seeds of his Spirit,
      let the fruit grow,
   tell the people of Jesus,
      let his love show.

2. Go through the park,
      on into the town;
   the sun still shines on
      it never goes down.
   The light of the world
      is risen again;
   the people of darkness
      are needing our friend.

3. Open your eyes,
      look into the sky,
   the darkness has come,
      the sun came to die.
   The evening draws on,
      the sun disappears,
   but Jesus is living,
      and his Spirit is near.

Sue McClellan, John Pac
and Keith Ryecroft

46

1. Come, adore this wondrous presence,
   bow to Christ, the source of grace.
   Here is kept the ancient promise
   of God's earthly dwelling-place.
   Sight is blind before God's glory,
   faith alone may see his face.

2. Glory be to God the Father,
   praise to his co-equal Son,
   adoration to the Spirit,
   bond of love, in Godhead one.
   Blest be God by all creation
   joyously while ages run.

   St Thomas Aquinas (1227-74)
   translated by James Quinn

47

1. Come, Christian people,
   take heed what I say:
   Here, in this stable,
   your King was born today.

   Star of wisdom, child of gladness,
   tell him all your troubles.
   Mary's boy has banished sadness,
   why be sorrowful now?

2. Not much to look at
   — simply straw and hay —
   yet on that carpet
   your King was laid today.

3. Man, are you listening?
   Take heed what I say:
   Here on this planet
   your King still lives today.

   John Glynn

48

Come, come, come to the manger,
children, come
to the children's King;
sing, sing, chorus of Angels,
stars of morning o'er Bethlehem sing.

1. He lies 'mid the beasts of the stall,
   who is Maker and Lord of us all;
   the wintry wind blows cold and
                              dreary,
   see, he weeps, the world is weary;
   Lord, have pity and mercy on me!

2. He leaves all his glory behind,
   to be born and to die for mankind,
   with grateful beasts his cradle
                              chooses,
   thankless man his love refuses;
   Lord, have pity and mercy on me!

3. To the manger of Bethlehem come,
   to the Saviour Emmanuel's home;
   the heav'nly hosts above are singing,
   set the Christmas bells a-ringing;
   Lord, have pity and mercy on me.

   Anonymous

49

1. Come down, O love divine,
   seek thou this soul of mine,
   and visit it with thine own
      ardour glowing;
   O comforter, draw near,
   within my heart appear,
   and kindle it, thy holy
      flame bestowing.

2. O let it freely burn,
   till earthly passions turn
   to dust and ashes in its
      heat consuming;
   and let thy glorious light
   shine ever on my sight,
   and clothe me round, the while my
      path illuming.

3. Let holy charity
   mine outward vesture be,
   and lowliness become mine
      inner clothing;
   true lowliness of heart,
   which takes the humbler part,
   and o'er its own shortcomings
      weeps with loathing.

4. And so the yearning strong,
   with which the soul will long,
   shall far outpass the power of
      human telling;
   for none can guess its grace,
   till he become the place
   wherein the Holy Spirit
   makes his dwelling.

Bianco da Siena d.1434,
tr. Richard Frederick Littledale

50

1. Come, Holy Ghost, Creator, come
   from thy bright heavenly throne,
   come, take possession of our souls,
   and make them all thine own.

2. Thou who art called the Paraclete,
   best gift of God above,
   the living spring, the living fire,
   sweet unction and true love.

3. Thou who are sev'nfold in thy grace,
   finger of God's right hand;
   his promise, teaching little ones
   to speak and understand.

4. O guide our minds with thy blest
      light,
   with love our hearts inflame;
   and with thy strength, which ne'er
      decays,
   confirm our mortal frame.

5. Far from us drive our deadly foe;
   true peace unto us bring;
   and through all perils lead us safe
   beneath thy sacred wing.

6. Through thee may we the Father
      know,
   through thee th'eternal Son,
   and thee the Spirit of them both,
   thrice-blessed Three in One.

7. All glory to the Father be,
   with his co-equal Son:
   the same to thee, great Paraclete,
   while endless ages run.

Ascribed to Rabanus Maurus (776-856)
tr. Anonymous

51

1. Come, Lord Jesus, come.
   Come, take my hands,
   take them for your work.
   Take them for your service Lord.
   Take them for your glory, Lord,
   Come, Lord Jesus, come.
   Come, Lord Jesus, take my hands.

2. Come, Lord Jesus, come.
   Come, take my eyes,
   may they shine with joy.
   Take them for your service, Lord.
   Take them for your glory, Lord.
   Come, Lord Jesus, come.
   Come, Lord Jesus, take my eyes.

3. Come, Lord Jesus, come.
   Come, take my lips,
   may they speak your truth.
   Take them for your service, Lord.
   Take them for your glory, Lord.
   Come, Lord Jesus, come.
   Come, Lord Jesus, take my lips.

4. Come, Lord Jesus, come.
   Come take my feet,
   may they walk your path.
   Take them for your service, Lord.
   Take them for your glory, Lord.
   Come, Lord Jesus, come.
   Come, Lord Jesus, take my feet.

5. Come, Lord Jesus, come.
   Come, take my heart,
   fill it with your love.
   Take it for your service, Lord.
   Take it for your glory, Lord.
   Come, Lord Jesus, come.
   Come, Lord Jesus, take my heart.

6. Come, Lord Jesus, come.
   Come, take my life,
   take it for your own.
   Take it for your service, Lord.
   Take it for your glory, Lord.
   Come, Lord Jesus, come.
   Come, Lord Jesus, take my life.

Kevin Mayhew

52

1. Come, my brothers, praise the Lord,
    alleluia.
  He's our God and we are his,
    alleluia.

2. Come to him with songs of praise,
    alleluia.
  Songs of praise, rejoice in him,
    alleluia.

3. For the Lord is a mighty God,
    alleluia.
  He is king of all the world,
    alleluia.

4. In his hands are valleys deep,
    alleluia.
  In his hands are mountain peaks,
    alleluia.

5. In his hands are all the seas,
    alleluia.
  And the lands which he has made,
    alleluia.

6. Praise the Father, praise the Son,
    alleluia.
  Praise the Spirit, the Holy One,
    alleluia.

Traditional

53

1. Come, praise the Lord, the almighty,
    the King of all nations!
  Tell forth his fame, O ye peoples,
    with loud acclamations!
      His love is sure;
        faithful his word shall endure,
  steadfast through all generations!

2. Praise to the Father most gracious,
    the Lord of creation!
  Praise to his Son, the Redeemer
    who wrought our salvation!
      O heav'nly Dove,
        praise to thee, fruit of their
          love.
  Giver of all consolation!

Psalm 116, versified by James Quinn

54

1. Come to the Lord
      and gather round his table.
    Gather round his table
      and come to the Lord.

2. Speak to the Lord
      and gather round his table.
    Gather round his table
      and speak to the Lord.

3. Sing to the Lord
      and gather round his table.
    Gather round his table
      and sing to the Lord.

4. Clap to the Lord
      and gather round his table.
    Gather round his table
      and clap to the Lord.

5. Dance to the Lord
      and gather round his table.
    Gather round his table
      and dance to the Lord.

Estelle White

55

1. Come, ye thankful people, come,
    raise the song of harvest-home!
  All be safely gathered in,
  ere the winter storms begin;
  God, our maker, doth provide
  for our wants to be supplied;
  come to God's own temple come;
  raise the song of harvest-home!

2. We ourselves are God's own field,
  fruit unto his praise to yield;
  wheat and tares together sown,
  unto joy or sorrow grown;
  first the blade and then the ear,
  then the full corn shall appear:
  grant, O harvest Lord, that we
  wholesome grain and pure may be.

3. For the Lord our God shall come,
   and shall take his harvest home;
   from his field shall purge away
   all that doth offend, that day,
   give his angels charge at last
   in the fire the tares to cast,
   but the fruitful ears to store
   in his garner evermore.

4. Then, thou Church triumphant,
                                come,
   raise the song of harvest-home;
   all be safely gathered in,
   free from sorrow, free from sin,
   there for ever purified
   in God's garner to abide:
   come, ten thousand angels, come,
   raise the glorious harvest-home!

   Henry Alford (1810-71)

56

1. Crown him with many crowns,
   the Lamb upon his throne;
   hark, how the heavenly anthem
                                drowns
   all music but its own:
   awake, my soul, and sing
   of him who died for thee,
   and hail him as thy matchless King
   through all eternity.

2. Crown him the Virgin's Son,
   the God incarnate born,
   whose arm those crimson trophies
                                won
   which now his brow adorn;
   fruit of the mystic rose,
   as of that rose the stem,
   the root, whence mercy ever flows,
   the babe of Bethlehem.

3. Crown him the Lord of love;
   behold his hands and side,
   rich wounds, yet visible above,
   in beauty glorified:
   no angel in the sky
   can fully bear that sight,
   but downward bends his burning eye
   at mysteries so bright.

4. Crown him the Lord of peace,
   whose power a sceptre sways,
   from pole to pole, that wars may
                                cease,
   absorbed in prayer and praise:
   his reign shall know no end,
   and round his pierced feet
   fair flowers of Paradise extend
   their fragrance ever sweet.

5. Crown him the Lord of heaven,
   one with the Father known,
   and the blest Spirit through him
                                given
   from yonder triune throne:
   all hail, Redeemer, hail,
   for thou hast died for me;
   thy praise shall never, never fail
   throughout eternity.

   Matthew Bridges (1800-94)

57

1. Daily, daily, sing to Mary,
   sing my soul, her praises due;
   all her feasts, her actions worship,
   with the heart's devotion true.
   Lost in wond'ring contemplation
   be her majesty confessed:
   call her Mother, call her Virgin,
   happy Mother, Virgin blest.

2. She is mighty to deliver;
   call her, trust her lovingly.
   When the tempest rages round thee,
   she will calm the troubled sea.
   Gifts of heaven she has given,
   noble Lady! to our race:
   she, the Queen, who decks her
                                subjects,
   with the light of God's own grace.

3. Sing, my tongue, the Virgin's
                                trophies,
   who for us her Maker bore;
   for the curse of old inflicted,
   peace and blessings to restore.
   Sing in songs of praise unending,
   sing the world's majestic Queen;
   weary not nor faint in telling
   all the gifts she gives to men.

4. All my senses, heart, affections,
   strive to sound her glory forth;
   spread abroad the sweet memorials,
   of the Virgin's priceless worth,
   where the voice of music thrilling,
   where the tongues of eloquence,
   that can utter hymns beseeming
   all her matchless excellence?

5. All our joys do flow from Mary,
   all then join her praise to sing;
   trembling sing the Virgin Mother,
   Mother of our Lord and King,
   while we sing her awful glory,
   far above our fancy's reach,
   let our hearts be quick to offer
   love the heart alone can teach.

*Ascribed to St. Bernard of Cluny
(12th c.), tr. Henry Bittleston*

58

*Day by day in the market place
I play my flute all day.
I have piped to them all,
   but nobody dances.
Day by day in the market place
I play my flute all day,
and whoever you be,
   won't you dance with me.*

1. At Cana, when my mother pleaded
   that they were short of wine,
   I gave them all the wine they needed;
   their happiness was mine.

2. Once, when I found poor Peter
   quaking,
   I let him walk the sea.
   I filled their fishing nets to breaking
   that day in Galilee.

3. While all the world despised the
   sinner
   I showed him hope again,
   and gave the honours at that dinner
   to Mary Magdalene.

4. Lazarus from the tomb advancing
   once more drew life's sweet breath.
   You too will leave the churchyard
   dancing,
   for I have conquered death.

Aimé Duval

59

1. Day is done, but Love unfailing
   dwells ever here;
   shadows fall, but hope, prevailing,
   calms every fear.
   Loving Father, none forsaking,
   take our hearts, of Love's own making,
   watch our sleeping, guard our waking,
   be always near!

2. Dark descends, but Light unending
   shines through our night;
   you are with us, ever lending
   new strength to sight;
   one in love, your truth confessing,
   one in hope of heaven's blessing,
   may we see, in love's possessing,
   love's endless light!

3. Eyes will close, but you, unsleeping,
   watch by our side;
   death may come: in love's safe keeping
   still we abide.
   God of love, all evil quelling,
   sin forgiving, fear dispelling,
   stay with us, our hearts indwelling,
   this eventide!

James Quinn

60

1. Dear Lord and Father of mankind,
   forgive our foolish ways!
   Re-clothe us in our rightful mind,
   in purer lives thy service find,
   in deeper reverence praise,
   in deeper reverence praise.

2. In simple trust like theirs who heard
   beside the Syrian sea,
   the gracious calling of the Lord,
   let us, like them, without a word,
   rise up and follow thee,
   rise up and follow thee.

3. O Sabbath rest by Galilee!
O calm of hills above,
where Jesus knelt to share with thee
the silence of eternity,
interpreted by love!
interpreted by love!

4. Drop thy still dews of quietness,
till all our strivings cease;
take from our souls the strain and
stress,
and let our ordered lives confess.
The beauty of thy peace.
The beauty of thy peace.

5. Breathe through the heats of our
desire
thy coolness and thy balm;
let sense be dumb, let flesh retire;
speak through the earthquake, wind
and fire,
O still small voice of calm!
O still small voice of calm!

John Greenleaf Whittier (1807-92)

61

1. Dear maker of the starry skies,
light of believers evermore,
Jesu, redeemer of mankind,
be near us who thine aid implore.

2. When man was sunk in sin and death,
lost in the depth of Satan's snare,
love brought thee down to cure our
ills,
by taking of those ills a share.

3. Thou for the sake of guilty men
permitting thy pure blood to flow,
didst issue from thy virgin shrine
and to the cross a victim go.

4. So great the glory of thy might,
if we but chance thy name to sound,
at once all heaven and hell unite
in bending low with awe profound.

5. Great judge of all, in that last day,
when friends shall fail and foes
combine,
be present then with us, we pray,
to guard us with thy arm divine.

6. To God the Father with the Son,
and Holy Spirit, one and three,
be honour, glory, blessing, praise,
all through the long eternity.

7th c., tr. Edward Caswall

62

1. Ding dong! merrily on high
in heav'n the bells are ringing,
ding dong! verily the sky
is riv'n with angels singing.

Gloria, hosanna in excelsis!

2. E'en so here below, below,
let steeple bells be swungen,
and io, io, io,
by priest and people sungen.

3. Pray you, dutifully prime
your matin chime, ye ringers;
may you beautifully rime
your evetime song, ye singers.

George Ratcliffe Woodward
(1848-1934)

63

Do not worry over what to eat,
what to wear or put upon your feet.
Trust and pray,
go do your best today,
then leave it in the hands
of the Lord.
Leave it in the hands of the Lord.

1. The lilies of the field,
they do not spin or weave,
yet Solomon was not
arrayed like one of these.
The birds of the air,
they do not sow or reap,
but God tends to them,
like a shepherd tends his sheep.

2. The Lord will guide you
   in his hidden way,
   show you what to do
   and tell you what to say.
   When you pray for rain,
   go build a dam to store
   ev'ry drop of water
   you have asked him for.

3. The Lord knows all your
   needs before you ask.
   Only trust in him
   for he will do the task
   of bringing in your life
   whatever you must know.
   He'll lead you through the darkness
   wherever you must go.

Sebastian Temple

64

1. Do you know that the Lord
   walks on earth?
   Do you know he is living here now?
   He is waiting for all men
   to recognise him here.
   Do you know that the Lord
   walks on earth?

2. Do you know that he walks
   in disguise?
   Do you know he's in crowds
   ev'rywhere?
   Every place that you go,
   you may find that he is there.
   Do you know that the Lord's
   in disguise?

3. Do you know that the Lord
   thirsts so much?
   Do you know that he's sitting
   in jail?
   Ev'rywhere he is hungry
   and naked in the cold.
   Do you know he's rejected
   without care?

4. Do you know he is crucified
   each day?
   Do you know that he suffers
   and dies?
   Ev'rywhere he is lonely
   and waiting for a call.
   Do you know he is sick
   all alone?

5. Do you know that he wants
   to be free?
   Do you know he wants help
   from you and me?
   He has need of our hands
   and our feet and hearts to serve.
   Do you know he can work
   through men?

6. Do you know that the Lord
   dwells in men?
   Do you know he resides
   in their hearts?
   His face is shining
   in everyone we meet.
   Do you know he's disguised
   as ev'ry man?

7. Do you know that the Lord
   walks on earth?
   Do you know he is living here now?
   He is waiting for all men
   to recognise him here.
   Do you know he's disguised
   as ev'ry man?

Sebastian Temple

65

1. Draw nigh, and take
   the body of our Lord;
   and drink the holy blood
   for you outpoured;
   saved by that body,
   hallowed by that blood,
   whereby refreshed
   we render thanks to God.

2. Salvation's giver,
   Christ the only Son,
   by that his cross and blood
   the victory won,
   offered was he for
   greatest and for least;
   himself the victim,
   and himself the priest.

3. Victims were offered
   by the law of old,
   that, in a type,
   celestial mysteries told.
   He, ransomer from
   death and light from shade,
   giveth his holy grace
   his saints to aid.

4. Approach ye then with
   faithful hearts sincere,
   and take the safeguard
   of salvation here,
   he that in this world
   rules his saints and shields,
   to all believers
   life eternal yields.

5. With heav'nly bread
   makes them that hunger whole,
   gives living waters
   to the thirsty soul,
   Alpha and Omega,
   to whom shall bow
   all nations at the doom,
   is with us now.

   From the Antiphonary of Bennchar
   (7th C.), tr. J. M. Neale

66

1. Dust, dust, and ashes
   lie over on my grave.
   Dust, dust and ashes
   lie over on my grave.
   Dust, dust and ashes
   lie over on my grave,
   and the Lord shall bear
   my spirit home,
   and the Lord shall bear
   my spirit home.

2 They crucified my saviour
   and nailed him to the cross. . .

3. And Mary came a-running,
   her saviour for to see. . .

4. The angels said: "He's not here,
   he's gone to Galilee. . .

5. He rose, he rose, he rose up,
   he rose up from the dead. . .

   Traditional

67

1. Eternal Father, strong to save,
   whose arm doth bind the restless
                               wave,
   who bidd'st the mighty ocean deep,
   it's own appointed limits keep:
   O hear us when we cry to thee
   For those in peril on the sea.

2. O Saviour, whose almighty word
   the winds and waves submissive
                               heard,
   who walkedst on the foaming deep
   and calm amid its rage didst sleep:
   O hear us when we cry to thee
   for those in peril on the sea.

3. O sacred Spirit, who didst brood
   upon the waters dark and rude,
   and bid their angry tumult cease,
   and give, for wild confusion, peace:
   O hear us when we cry to thee
   for those in peril on the sea.

4. O Trinity of love and power,
   our brethren shield in danger's hour.
   From rock and tempest, fire and foe,
   protect them whereso'er they go,
   and ever let there rise to thee
   glad hymns of praise from land and
                               sea.

   W. Whiting (1825-78)

68

1. Faith of our fathers, living still
   in spite of dungeon, fire and sword;
   oh, how our hearts
   beat high with joy
   when e'er we hear that glorious
   word!

   Faith of our fathers! Holy Faith!
   We will be true to thee till death,
   we will be true to thee till death.

2. Our fathers, chained in prisons dark,
   were still in heart
   and conscience free;
   how sweet would be their children's
   fate,
   if they, like them, could die for thee!

3. Faith of our fathers, Mary's prayers,
   shall win our country back to thee;
   and through the truth
   that comes from God
   England shall then indeed be free.

4. Faith of our fathers, we will love
   both friend and foe in all our strife,
   and preach thee too,
   as love knows how.
   by kindly words and virtuous life.

   Frederick William Faber (1814-63)

69

1. Father and life-giver,
   grace of Christ impart;
   he, the word incarnate –
   food for mind and heart.
   Children of the promise,
   homage now we pay;
   sacrificial banquet
   cheers the desert way.

2. Wine and bread the symbols –
   love and life convey,
   offered by your people,
   work and joy portray.
   All we own consigning,
   nothing is retained;
   tokens of our service,
   gifts and song contain.

3. Transformation wondrous –
   water into wine;
   mingled in the Godhead
   we are made divine:
   Birth into his body
   brought us life anew,
   total consecration –
   fruit from grafting true.

4. Christ, the head and members
   living now as one,
   offered to the Father
   by this holy Son;
   and our adoration
   purified we find,
   through the Holy Spirit
   breathing in mankind.

   A. J. Newman

70

1. Father most holy,
   merciful and loving,
   Jesu, redeemer,
   ever to be worshipped,
   life-giving Spirit,
   Comforter most gracious,
   God everlasting.

2. Three in a wondrous
   unity unbroken,
   one perfect Godhead,
   love that never faileth,
   light of the angels,
   succour of the needy,
   hope of all living.

3. All thy creation
   serveth its creator,
   thee every creature
   praiseth without ceasing,
   we too would sing
   the psalms of true devotion:
   hear, we beseech thee.

4. Lord God almighty,
   unto thee be glory,
   one in three persons,
   over all exalted.
   Thine, as is meet,
   be honour, praise and blessing
   now and forever.

   10th c., tr. A. E. Alston

71

1. Father, within thy house today
   we wait thy kindly love to see:
   since thou hast said in truth that
                                    they
   who dwell in love are one with thee,
   bless those who for thy blessing
                                    wait;
   their love accept and consecrate.

2. Blest Spirit, who with life and light
   didst quicken chaos to thy praise,
   whose energy, in sin's despite,
   still lifts our nature up to grace,
   bless those who here in troth
                                consent,
   Creator, crown thy sacrament.

3. Great one in three, of whom are
                                named
   all families in earth and heaven,
   hear us, who have thy promise
                                claimed,
   and let a wealth of grace be given,
   grant them in life and death to be
   each knit to each, and both to thee.

   Robert Hugh Benson (1871-1914)

72

Feed us now, O Son of God,
as you fed them long ago.

1. The people came to hear you,
   the poor, the lame, the blind.
   They asked for food to save them,
   you fed them body and mind.

2. The ones who didn't listen,
   the rich, the safe, the sure,
   they didn't think they needed
   the offering of a cure.

3. It's hard for us to listen,
   things haven't changed at all.
   We've got the things we wanted;
   we don't want to hear your call.

4. Yet millions still have hunger,
   disease, no homes, and fear.
   We offer them so little,
   and it costs them very dear.

5. So help us see the writing,
   written clear upon the wall:
   he who doesn't feed his neighbour
   will get no food at all.

   Peter Allen

73

1. Fight the good fight with all thy
                                    might,
   Christ is thy strength, and Christ
                                    thy right;
   lay hold on life and it shall be
   thy joy and crown eternally.

2. Run the straight race through God's
                                    good grace,
   lift up thine eyes and seek his face;
   life with its way before us lies,
   Christ is the path, and Christ the
                                    prize.

3. Cast care aside, upon thy Guide
   lean, and his mercy will provide
   lean, and the trusting soul shall prove
   Christ is its life, and Christ its love.

4. Faint not nor fear, his arms are near,
   he changeth not, and thou art dear;
   only believe, and thou shalt see
   that Christ is all in all to thee.

   J. S. B. Monsell (1811-75)

74

1. Fill my house unto the fullest.
   Eat my bread and drink my wine.
   The love I bear is held from no-one.

   All I own
   and all I do
   I give to you.

2. Take my time unto the fullest.
   Find in me the trust you seek,
   and take my hands to you
                            outreaching.

3. Christ our Lord with love enormous
   from the cross his lesson taught
   – to love all men as I have loved you.

4. Join with me as one in Christ-love.
   May our hearts all beat as one,
   and may we give ourselves
   completely.

   Peter Kearney

75

1. Firmly I believe and truly
   God is three, and God is one,
   and I next acknowledge duly
   manhood taken by the Son.

2. And I trust and hope must fully
   in that manhood crucified;
   and each thought and deed unruly
   do to death, as he has died.

3. Simply to his grace and wholly
   light and life and strength belong;
   and I love supremely, solely,
   him the holy, him the strong.

4. And I hold in veneration,
   for the love of him alone,
   Holy Church, as his creation,
   and her teachings, as his own.

5. Adoration aye be given,
   with and through the angelic host,
   to the God of earth and heaven,
   Father, Son and Holy Ghost.

   John Henry Newman (1801-90)

76

1. Follow Christ and love the world
   as he did,
   when he walked upon the earth.
   Love each friend and enemy
   as he did.
   In God's eyes we have equal worth.

2. Follow Christ and serve the world
   as he did
   when he ministered to ev'ryone.
   Serve each friend and enemy
   as he did
   so that the Father's will be done.

3. He said: "Love each other
   as I love you.
   By this all men will know you're mine.
   As I served you I ask that you do.
   This new commandment I assign."

4. Follow Christ and love the world
   as he did
   when he walked upon the earth.
   Love each friend and enemy
   as he did.
   In God's eyes we have equal worth.

   Sebastian Temple

77

1. For all the saints
   who from their labours rest,
   who thee by faith
   before the world confest,
   thy name, O Jesus
   be for ever blest.

   Alleluia, alleluia!

2. Thou wast their rock,
   their fortress, and their might;
   thou, Lord, their captain
   in the well-fought fight;
   thou in the darkness drear
   their one true light.

3. O may thy soldiers,
   faithful, true, and bold,
   fight as the saints who
   nobly fought of old,
   and win, with them,
   the victor's crown of gold.

4. O blest communion!
   fellowship divine!
   We feebly struggle,
   they in glory shine;
   yet all are one in thee,
   for all are thine.

5. And when the strife is fierce,
   the warfare long,
   steals on the ear the
   distant triumph-song,
   and hearts are brave again,
   and arms are strong.

6. The golden evening
     brightens in the west;
   soon, soon to faithful
     warriors cometh rest:
   sweet is the calm of
     paradise the blest.

7. But lo! there breaks a
     yet more glorious day;
   the saints triumphant
     rise in bright array:
   the king of glory
     passes on his way.

8. From earth's wide bounds,
     from ocean's farthest coast,
   through gates of pearl streams
     in the countless host,
   singing to Father,
     Son and Holy Ghost.

   William Walsham How (1823-97)

78

1. Forth in the peace of Christ we go;
   Christ to the world with joy
     we bring;
   Christ in our minds, Christ on
     our lips,
   Christ in our hearts, the world's
     true King.

2. King of our hearts, Christ makes
     us kings;
   kingship with him his servants gain;
   with Christ, the Servant-Lord of all,
   Christ's world we serve to share
     Christ's reign.

3. Priests of the world, Christ sends
     us forth
   the world of time to consecrate,
   the world of sin by grace to heal,
   Christ's world in Christ to re-create.

4. Christ's are our lips, his word we
     speak;
   prophets are we whose deeds
     proclaim
   Christ's truth in love that we may be
   Christ in the world, to spread
     Christ's name.

5. We are the Church; Christ bids
     us show
   that in his Church all nations find
   their hearth and home where
     Christ restores
   true peace, true love, to all mankind.

   James Quinn, S.J.

79

1. Forth in thy name, O Lord, I go,
   my daily labour to pursue;
   thee, only thee, resolved to know,
   in all I think or speak or do.

2. The task thy wisdom hath assigned
   O let me cheerfully fulfil;
   in all my works thy presence find,
   and prove thy good and perfect will.

3. Thee may I set at my right hand,
   whose eyes my inmost substance
     see,
   and labour on at thy command,
   and offer all my works to thee.

4. Give me to bear thy easy yoke,
   and every moment watch and pray,
   and still to things eternal look,
   and hasten to thy glorious day;

5. For thee delightfully employ
   whate'er thy bounteous grace hath
     given,
   and run my course with even joy,
   and closely walk with thee to
     heaven.

   Charles Wesley (1707-88)

80

1. Forty days and forty nights
   thou wast fasting in the wild;
   forty days and forty nights
   tempted still, yet unbeguiled:

2. Sunbeams scorching all the day,
   chilly dew-drops nightly shed,
   prowling beasts about thy way,
   stones thy pillow, earth thy bed.

3. Let us thy endurance share
   and from earthly greed abstain
   with thee watching unto prayer,
   with thee strong to suffer pain.

4. Then if evil on us press,
   flesh or spirit to assail,
   victor in the wilderness,
   help us not to swerve or fail!

5. So shall peace divine be ours;
   holier gladness ours shall be,
   come to us angelic powers,
   such as ministered to thee.

6. Keep, O keep us, Saviour dear,
   ever constant by thy side,
   that with thee we may appear
   at the eternal Eastertide.

   George Hunt Smyttan (1822-70)
   and others

81

1. From the deep I lift my voice,
   hear my cry, O God;
   listen, Lord, to my appeal,
   none but you can help.

2. If you count our grievous sins,
   no man will be spared,
   but your mercy still forgives,
   in your love we trust.

3. Night and day my spirit waits,
   longs to see my God,
   like a watchman, weary, cold,
   waiting for the dawn.

4. Open-handed is the Lord,
   swift to pardon us:
   he will lead his people free,
   clean from all their sins.

5. Glory be to God our Lord,
   merciful and kind,
   Father, Son and Holy Ghost,
   now and evermore.

   Paraphrased from Psalm 129
   by Luke Connaughton

82

1. From the depths we cry to thee,
   God of sovereign majesty!
   Hear our chants and hymns of
                                 praise;
   bless our Lent of forty days.

2. Though our consciences proclaim
   our transgressions and our shame,
   cleanse us, Lord, we humbly plead,
   from our sins of thought and deed.

3. Lord, accept our Lenten fast
   and forgive our sinful past,
   that we may partake with thee
   in the Easter mystery.

   Based on Psalm 129
   by Sister M. Teresine

83

1. Give me peace, O Lord, I pray,
   in my work and in my play,
   and inside my heart and mind,
   Lord, give me peace.

2. Give peace to the world, I pray,
   let all quarrels cease today.
   May we spread your light and love.
   Lord, give us peace.

   Estelle White

84

1. Give me joy in my heart,
        keep me praising,
   give me joy in my heart I pray.
   Give me joy in my heart
        keep me praising.
   Keep me praising till the end of day.

   Sing hosanna! Sing hosanna!
   Sing hosanna to the King of Kings!
   Sing hosanna! Sing hosanna!
   Sing hosanna to the King!

2. Give me peace in my heart,
        keep me resting,
   give me peace in my heart I pray.
   Give me peace in my heart,
        keep me resting.
   Keep me resting till the end of day.

3. Give me love in my heart,
     keep me serving,
   give me love in my heart, I pray.
   Give me love in my heart,
     keep me serving,
   keep me serving 'till the end of day.

Traditional

85

1. Give me yourself
     O Jesus Christ my brother,
   give me yourself
     O Jesus Christ my Lord.

2. Give me your peace,
     O Jesus Christ my brother,
   give me your peace,
     O Jesus Christ my Lord.

3. Give me your love,
     O Jesus Christ my brother,
   give me your love,
     O Jesus Christ my Lord.

4. Give me your heart,
     O Jesus Christ my brother,
   give me your heart,
     O Jesus Christ my Lord.

Estelle White

86

1. Glorious God, King of creation,
   we praise you, we bless you,
     we worship you in song.
   Glorious God, in adoration,
   at your feet we belong.

   Lord of life, Father almighty,
   Lord of hearts, Christ the King.
   Lord of love, Holy Spirit,
   to whom we homage bring.

2. Glorious God, magnificent, holy,
   we love you, adore you,
     and come to you in pray'r.
   Glorious God, mighty, eternal,
   we sing your praise ev'rywhere.

Sebastian Temple

87

Glory be to God, the King of kings.
Hosanna, hosanna!
Raise your voices
let the whole world sing.
Hosanna, hosanna.

1. Praise him sun and moon and all that
     gives the world its light,
   planets and the galaxies and
   shooting stars at night.

2. Butterflies and silken moths and
     spiders in their webs,
   praise him streams and rounded
                                 stones that
   line a river bed.

3. Praise him concrete, glass and steel
     that form a city's face,
   piston rods and generators,
   satellites in space.

4. Praise him all the oceans and the
     waves upon the shore,
   albatross and kittiwake and
   seagulls as they soar.

5. Praise him all you people from the
     near and distant lands,
   praise him for the fruitful earth,
   his loving gift to man.

   Glory be to God, the King of kings.
   Hosanna, hosanna!
   Raise your voices
     let the whole world sing.
   Hosanna, hosanna, hosanna,
     hosanna, hosanna.

Estelle White

88

1. Glory be to Jesus,
   who in bitter pains
   poured for me the life-blood,
   from his sacred veins.

2. Grace and life eternal
   in that blood I find:
   blest be his compassion,
   infinitely kind.

3. Blest through endless ages
   be the precious stream,
   which from endless torment
   doth the world redeem.

4. There the fainting spirit
   drinks of life her fill;
   there as in a fountain
   laves herself at will.

5. Abel's blood for vengeance
   pleaded to the skies,
   but the blood of Jesus
   for our pardon cries.

6. Oft as it is sprinkled
   on our guilty hearts,
   Satan in confusion
   terror-struck departs.

7. Oft as earth exulting
   wafts its praise on high,
   hell with horror trembles;
   heaven is filled with joy.

8. Lift ye, then, your voices;
   swell the mighty flood;
   louder still and louder,
   praise the precious blood.

   18th c., tr. Edward Caswall

89

1. Glory to God, glory to God,
   glory to the Father.
   Glory to God, glory to God,
   glory to the Father.
   To him be glory for ever.
   To him be glory for ever.
   Alleluia, amen.
   Alleluia, amen,
   alleluia, amen,
   alleluia, amen.

2. Glory to God, glory to God,
   Son of the Father.
   Glory to God, glory to God,
   Son of the Father.
   To him be glory for ever.
   To him be glory for ever.
   Alleluia, amen.
   Alleluia, amen,
   alleluia, amen,
   alleluia, amen.

3. Glory to God, glory to God,
   glory to the Spirit.
   Glory to God, glory to God,
   glory to the Spirit.
   To him be glory for ever.
   To him be glory for ever.
   Alleluia, amen.
   Alleluia, amen,
   alleluia, amen,
   alleluia, amen.

   Peruvian

90

1. Glory to thee, Lord God!
   in faith and hope we sing.
   Through this completed sacrifice
   our love and praise we bring.
   We give thee for our sins
   a price beyond all worth,
   which none could ever fitly pay
   but this thy Son on earth.

2. Here is the Lord of all,
   to thee in glory slain;
   of worthless givers, worthy gift
   a victim without stain.
   Through him we give thee thanks,
   with him we bend the knee,
   in him be all our life, who is
   our one true way to thee.

3. So may this sacrifice
   we offer here this day,
   be joined with our poor lives in all
   we think and do and say.
   By living true to grace,
   for thee and thee alone,
   our sorrows, labours, and our joys
   will be his very own.

John Greally

91

1. Glory to thee, my God, this night
   for all the blessings of the light;
   keep me, O keep me, King of kings,
   beneath thy own almighty wings.

2. Forgive me, Lord, for thy dear Son,
   the ill that I this day have done,
   that with the world, myself and
   thee,
   I, ere I sleep, at peace may be.

3. Teach me to live, that I may dread
   the grave as little as my bed;
   teach me to die, that so I may
   rise glorious at the awful day.

4. O may my soul on thee repose,
   and with sweet sleep mine eyelids
   close,
   sleep that may me more vigorous
   make
   to serve my God when I awake.

5. Praise God, from whom all blessings
   flow;
   praise him, all creatures here below;
   praise him above, ye heavenly host;
   praise Father, Son, and Holy Ghost.

T. Ken (1637-1711)

92

*Go, tell it on the mountain,
over the hills and ev'rywhere.
Go, tell it on the mountain
that Jesus Christ is born.*

1. While shepherds kept their watching
   o'er wand'ring flocks by night,
   behold from out of heaven
   there shone a holy light.

2. And lo, when they had seen it,
   they all bowed down and prayed,
   they travelled on together
   to where the Babe was laid.

3. When I was a seeker,
   I sought both night and day:
   I asked my Lord to help me
   and he showed me the way.

4. He made me a watchman
   upon the city wall,
   And if I am a Christian,
   I am the least of all.

Traditional

93

1. God be in my head, and in my
   understanding,
   God be in mine eyes, and in my
   looking,
   God be in my mouth, and in my
   speaking,
   God be in my heart, and in my
   thinking,
   God be at mine end, and at my
   departing.

Book of Hours (1514)

94

1. God everlasting, wonderful,
    and holy,
  Father most gracious,
      we who stand before thee
  here at thine altar,
      as thy Son has taught us,
  come to adore thee.

2. Countless the mercies thou hast
      lavished on us,
  source of all blessing
      to all creatures living;
  to thee we render,
      for thy love o'erflowing.
  Humble thanksgiving.

3. Now in remembrance of our
      great redeemer,
  dying on Calvary,
      rising and ascending,
  through him we offer
      what he ever offers,
  sinners befriending.

4. Strength to the living,
      rest to the departed,
  grant, Holy Father,
      through this pure oblation:
  may the life-giving
      bread for ever bring us
  health and salvation.

Harold Riley

95

1. Godhead here in hiding,
      whom I do adore,
  masked by these bare shadows,
      shape and nothing more,
  see, Lord, at thy service
      low lies here a heart
  lost, all lost in wonder
      at the God thou art.

2. Seeing, touching, tasting
      are in thee deceived;
  how says trusty hearing?
      That shall be believed;
  what God's Son hath told me,
      take for truth I do;
  truth himself speaks truly,
      or there's nothing true.

3. On the cross thy Godhead
      made no sign to men;
  here thy very manhood
      steals from human ken;
  both are my confession,
      both are my belief;
  and I pray the prayer
      of the dying thief.

4. I am not like Thomas,
      wounds I cannot see,
  but can plainly call thee
      Lord and God as he;
  this faith each day deeper
      be my holding of,
  daily make me harder
      hope and dearer love.

5. O thou our reminder
      of Christ crucified,
  living Bread, the life of
      us for whom he died,
  lend this life to me then;
      feed and feast my mind,
  there be thou the sweetness
      man was meant to find.

6. Jesu, whom I look at
      shrouded here below,
  I beseech thee send me
      what I long for so,
  some day to gaze on thee
      face to face in light
  and be blest for ever
      with thy glory's sight.

*Ascribed to St. Thomas Aquinas
(1227-74), tr. Gerard Manley Hopkins*

96

1. God is love
   and the one who lives in love
   lives in God,
   and God lives in him.
   And we have come to know
   and have believed
   the love which God has for us.
   God is love
   and the one who lives in love
   lives in God,
   and God lives in him.

2. God is hope . . .

3. God is peace . . .

4. God is joy . . .

Anonymous

97

1. God is love: his the care,
   tending each, everywhere.
   God is love, all is there!
   Jesus came to show him,
   that mankind might know him!

   Sing aloud, loud, loud!
   Sing aloud, loud, loud!
   God is good!
   God is truth! God is beauty!
   Praise him!

2. None can see God above;
   all have here man to love;
   thus may we Godward move,
   finding him in others,
   holding all men brothers:

3. Jesus lived here for men:
   strove and died, rose again,
   rules our hearts, now as then;
   for he came to save us
   by the truth he gave us:

4. To our Lord praise we sing,
   light and life, friend and king,
   coming down love to bring,
   pattern for our duty,
   showing God in beauty:

Percy Dearmer (1867-1936)

98

1. God of mercy and compassion,
   look with pity upon me;
   Father, let me call thee Father,
   'tis thy child returns to thee.

   Jesus Lord, I ask for mercy;
   let me not implore in vain:
   all my sins I now detest them,
   never will I sin again.

2. By my sins I have deserved
   death and endless misery,
   hell with all its pain and torments,
   and for all eternity.

3. By my sins I have abandon'd
   right and claim to heaven above,
   where the saints rejoice for ever,
   in a boundless sea of love.

4. See our Saviour, bleeding, dying,
   on the cross of Calvary;
   to that cross my sins have nail'd
                                    him,
   yet he bleeds and dies for me.

E. Vaughan (1827-1908)

99

1. God's spirit is in my heart.
   He has called me and set me apart.
   This is what I have to do,
   what I have to do.

   He sent me to give
       the Good News to the poor,
   tell prisoners that they are
       prisoners no more,
   tell blind people that they can see,
   and set the downtrodden free,
   and go tell ev'ryone
   the news that the Kingdom of God
       has come,
   and go tell ev'ryone
   the news that God's kingdom
       has come.

2. Just as the Father sent me,
   so I'm sending you out to be
   my witnesses throughout the world,
   the whole of the world.

3. Don't carry a load in your pack,
   you don't need two shirts on your
                                    back.
   A workman can earn his own keep,
   can earn his own keep.

4. Don't worry what you have to say,
   don't worry because on that day
   God's spirit will speak in your heart,
   will speak in your heart.

Alan Dale

100

1. Going home, going home,
   I'm a-going home.
   Quiet like, some still day,
   I'm just going home.
   It's not far, just close by,
   through an open door.
   Work all done, care laid by,
   going to fear no more.
   Mother's there expecting me,
   father's waiting too.
   Lots of folk gathered there,
   all the friends I knew,
   all the friends I knew.

2. Morning star lights the way,
   restless dreams all done.
   Shadows gone, break of day,
   real life just begun.
   There's no break, there's no end,
   just a living on,
   wide awake, with a smile,
   going on and on.
   Going home, going home,
   I'm just going home.
   It's not far, just close by,
   through an open door.
   I'm just going home.

William Arms Fisher

101

1. Gonna lay down
      my sword and shield
   down by the riverside,
   down by the riverside,
   down by the riverside,
   Gonna lay down
      my sword and shield
   down by the riverside.
   I ain't gonna study war no more.

   I ain't gonna study war no more.

2. Gonna walk with
      the Prince of Peace
   down by the riverside,
   down by the riverside,
   down by the riverside.
   Gonna walk with
      the Prince of Peace
   down by the riverside.
   I ain't gonna study war no more.

3. Gonna shake hands
      around the world
   down by the riverside,
   down by the riverside,
   down by the riverside.
   Gonna shake hands
      around the world
   down by the riverside.
   I ain't gonna study war no more.

Traditional Spiritual

102

1. Go, the Mass is ended,
   children of the Lord.
   Take his Word to others
   as you've heard it spoken to you.
   Go, the Mass is ended,
   go and tell the world
   the Lord is good, the Lord is kind,
   and he loves ev'ryone.

2. Go, the Mass is ended,
   take his love to all.
   Gladden all who meet you,
   fill their hearts with hope and
                                   courage.
   Go, the Mass is ended,
   fill the world with love,
   and give to all what you've received
   — the peace and joy of Christ.

3. Go, the Mass is ended,
   strengthened in the Lord,
   lighten ev'ry burden,
   spread the joy of Christ around you.
   Go, the Mass is ended,
   take his peace to all.
   This day is yours to change the
                                   world
   — to make God known and loved.

   Sister Marie Lydia Pereira

103

1. Great Saint Andrew, friend of Jesus,
   lover of his glorious cross,
   early by his voice effective
   called from ease to pain and loss,
   strong Saint Andrew, Simon's
                                   brother,
   who with haste fraternal flew,
   fain with him to share the treasure
   which, at Jesus' lips, he drew.

2. Blest Saint Andrew, Jesus' herald,
   true apostle, martyr bold,
   who, by deeds his words confirming,
   sealed with blood the truth he told.
   Ne'er to king was crown so
                                   beauteous,
   ne'er was prize to heart so dear,
   as to him the cross of Jesus
   when its promised joys drew near.

3. Loved Saint Andrew, Scotland's
                                   patron,
   watch thy land with heedful eye,
   rally round the cross of Jesus
   all her storied chivalry!
   To the Father, Son, and Spirit,
   fount of sanctity and love,
   give we glory, now and ever,
   with the saints who reign above.

   Frederick Oakeley (1802-80)

104

1. Guide me, O thou great redeemer,
   pilgrim through this barren land;
   I am weak, but thou art mighty,
   hold me with thy powerful hand:
   Bread of heaven,
   feed me till I want no more.

2. Open now the crystal fountain,
   whence the healing stream doth
                                   flow;
   let the fire and cloudy pillar
   lead me all my journey through;
   strong Deliverer.
   be thou still my strength and shield.

3. When I tread the verge of Jordan,
   bid my anxious fears subside,
   death of death, and hell's
                                   destruction,
   land me safe on Canaan's side;
   songs of praises,
   I will ever give to thee.

   W. Williams (1717-91),
   tr. P. and W. Williams

105

1. Hail, glorious Saint Patrick,
    dear saint of our isle,
   on us thy poor children
    bestow a sweet smile;
   and now thou art high
    in the mansions above,
   on Erin's green valleys
   look down in thy love.
   On Erin's green valleys,
    on Erin's green valleys,
   on Erin's green valleys
    look down in thy love.

2. Hail, glorious Saint Patrick!
    thy words were once strong
   against Satan's wiles and
    an infidel throng;
   not less is thy might
    where in heaven thou art;
   O, come to our aid,
    in our battle take part.

3. In the war against sin,
    in the fight for the faith,
   dear saint, may thy children
    resist unto death;
   may their strength be in meekness,
    in penance, in prayer,
   Their banner the Cross
    which they glory to bear.

4. Thy people, now exiles
    on many a shore,
   shall love and revere thee
    till time be no more;
   and the fire thou hast kindled
    shall ever burn bright,
   Its warmth undiminished,
    undying its light.

5. Ever bless and defend the sweet
    land of our birth,
   where the shamrock still blooms
    as when thou wert on earth,
   and our hearts shall yet burn,
    wheresoever we roam,
   For God and Saint Patrick,
    and our native home.

   Sister Agnes

106

1. Hail, Queen of heav'n, the ocean
   star,
    guide of the wand'rer here below;
   thrown on life's surge, we claim thy
   care;
    save us from peril and from woe.
   Mother of Christ, star of the sea,
   pray for the wanderer, pray for me.

2. O gentle, chaste and spotless maid,
    we sinners make our prayers
   through thee;
    remind thy son that he has paid
   the price of our iniquity.
   Virgin most pure, star of the sea,
   pray for the sinner, pray for me.

3. Sojourners in this vale of tears,
    to thee, blest advocate, we cry;
   pity our sorrows, calm our fears,
    and soothe with hope our misery.
   Refuge in grief, star of the sea,
   pray for the mourner, pray for me.

4. And while to him who reigns above,
    in Godhead One, in Persons Three,
   the source of life, of grace, of love,
    homage we pay on bended knee,
   do thou, bright Queen, star of the
   sea,
    pray for thy children, pray for me.

   John Lingard (1771-1851)

107

1. Hail, Redeemer, King divine!
   Priest and Lamb, the throne is thine.
   King, whose reign shall never cease,
   Prince of everlasting peace.

   Angels, saints and nations sing:
   'Praised be Jesus Christ, our King;
   Lord of life, earth, sky and sea,
   King of love on Calvary.'

2. King whose name creation thrills,
   rule our minds, our hearts, our wills
   till in peace each nation rings
   with thy praises, King of kings.

3. King most holy, King of truth,
   guide the lowly, guide the youth;
   Christ thou King of glory bright,
   be to us eternal light.

4. Shepherd-King, o'er mountains steep,
   homeward bring the wandering
                              sheep,
   shelter in one royal fold
   states and kingdoms, new and old.

Patrick Brennan

8. Ever upward let us move,
   wafted on the wings of love;
   looking when our Lord shall come,
   longing, sighing after home.

*Charles Wesley (1707-88), Thomas
Cotterill (1779-1823) and others*

108

1. Hail the day that sees him rise,
                              alleluia!
   To his throne above the skies;
                              alleluia!
   Christ, the Lamb for sinners given,
                              alleluia!
   Enters now the highest heaven,
                              alleluia!

2. There for him high triumph waits,
   lift your heads, eternal gates!
   He hath conquered death and sin;
   take the king of glory in!

3. Circled round with angel-powers,
   their triumphant Lord and ours;
   wide unfold the radiant scene,
   take the king of glory in!

4. Lo, the heaven its Lord receives,
   yet he loves the earth he leaves;
   though returning to his throne,
   still he calls mankind his own.

5. See! he lifts his hands above,
   see! he shows the prints of love;
   hark! his gracious lips bestow,
   blessings on his Church below.

6. Still for us he intercedes,
   his prevailing death he pleads;
   near himself prepares our place,
   he the first-fruits of our race.

7. Lord, though parted from our sight,
   far above the starry height,
   grant our hearts may thither rise,
   seeking thee above the skies.

109

1. Hail, thou star of ocean,
   portal of the sky;
   ever virgin Mother
   of the Lord most high.
   Oh! by Gabriel's Ave,
   utter'd long ago,
   Eva's name reversing,
   'stablish peace below.

2. Break the captive's fetters,
   light on blindness pour,
   all our ills expelling,
   every bliss implore.
   Show thyself a mother;
   offer him our sighs,
   who for us incarnate
   did not thee despise.

3. Virgin of all virgins,
   to thy shelter take us;
   gentlest of the gentle,
   chaste and gentle make us.
   Still, as on we journey,
   help our weak endeavour;
   till with thee and Jesus
   we rejoice for ever.

4. Through the highest heaven,
   to the almighty Three,
   Father, Son and Spirit,
   One same glory be.

9th c., tr. Edward Caswall

110

1. Hail to the Lord's anointed!
   Great David's greater son;
   hail, in the time appointed,
   his reign on earth begun!
   he comes to break oppression,
   to set the captive free;
   to take away transgression,
   and rule in equity.

2. He shall come down like showers
   upon the fruitful earth,
   and love, joy, hope, like flowers,
   spring in his path to birth:
   before him on the mountains
   shall peace the herald go;
   and righteousness in fountains
   from hill to valley flow.

3. Kings shall fall down before him,
   and gold and incense bring;
   all nations shall adore him,
   his praise all people sing,
   to him shall prayer unceasing
   and daily vows ascend;
   his kingdom still increasing
   a kingdom without end.

4. O'er every foe victorious,
   he on his throne shall rest,
   from age to age more glorious,
   all-blessing and all-blest;
   the tide of time shall never
   his covenant remove;
   his name shall stand for ever;
   that name to us is love.

   James Montgomery (1771-1854)

111

Happy the man
   who wanders with the Lord.
Happy the man
   who knows how to live.
Happy the man
   who never seeks reward,
giving because he loves to give.
He seeks no gold, he wants no gain.

He knows those things
   are all in vain.
He needs no praise nor honour, too.
His only motto:
   'To your own self be true.'
Happy the man
   who learned how to pray.
Happy the man
   who has a burning goal.
Happy the man
   whose service needs no pay.
This man has found his own soul.
Happy the man,
   happy the man of the Lord.

   Sebastian Temple

112

1. Hark! a herald voice is calling:
   'Christ is nigh' it seems to say;
   'Cast away the dreams of darkness,
   O ye children of the day!'

2. Startled at the solemn warning,
   let the earth-bound soul arise;
   Christ, her sun, all sloth dispelling,
   shines upon the morning skies.

3. Lo! the Lamb, so long expected,
   comes with pardon down from
                              heaven;
   let us haste, with tears of sorrow,
   one and all to be forgiven;

4. So when next he comes with glory,
   wrapping all the earth in fear,
   may he then as our defender
   on the clouds of heaven appear.

5. Honour, glory, virtue, merit,
   to the Father and the Son,
   with the co-eternal Spirit,
   while unending ages run.

   6th c., tr. Edward Caswall

113

1. Hark, the herald angels sing,
   glory to the new-born King;
   peace on earth and mercy mild,
   God and sinners reconciled:
   joyful all ye nations rise,
   join the triumph of the skies,
   with the angelic host proclaim,
   Christ is born in Bethlehem.

   Hark, the herald Angels sing,
   glory to the new-born King.

2. Christ, by highest heaven adored,
   Christ, the everlasting Lord,
   late in time behold him come,
   offspring of a Virgin's womb!
   Veiled in flesh the Godhead see,
   hail the incarnate Deity!
   Pleased as man with man to dwell,
   Jesus, our Emmanuel.

3. Hail the heaven-born Prince of
                          peace!
   Hail the Son of Righteousness!
   Light and life to all he brings
   risen with healing in his wings;
   mild he lays his glory by,
   born that man no more may die,
   born to raise the sons of earth,
   born to give them second birth.

   Charles Wesley (1743),
   George Whitefield (1753),
   Martin Madan (1760), and others

114

Haul, haul away.
Haul, haul away.
Cast the nets wide
    and sink the nets deep
and it's haul, haul away.

1. Oh, he sat in the boat
      and he spoke to the crowd.
   Haul, haul away.
   And his voice wasn't soft
      and his voice wasn't loud.
   Haul, haul away.
   And he spoke of the just
      and the pure and the free,
   and his voice caught the air
      like a net in the sea.
   And it's . . .

2. He said; "Cast your nets wide
      where the water is deep."
   Haul, haul away.
   "Oh, cast the nets wide
      and sink the nets deep."
   Haul, haul away.
   "Though we've worked through the
   night and we've nothing to show,
   we will try once again
      just because you say so."
   And it's . . .

3. Oh the catch it was huge
      and the boat it was small.
   Haul, haul away.
   His friends came to help
      when they heard Peter call.
   Haul, haul away.
   "You must leave us," said Peter,
      "for we're men of sin."
   But he said: "Come with me
      and be fishers of men."
   And it's . . .

   Michael Cockett

115

1. Help, Lord, the souls that thou hast
                                    made,
      the souls to thee so dear,
   in prison for the debt unpaid
   of sin committed here.

2. These holy souls, they suffer on,
   resigned in heart and will,
   until thy high behest is done,
   and justice has its fill.

3. For daily falls, for pardoned crime
they joy to undergo
the shadow of thy cross sublime,
the remnant of thy woe.

4. Oh, by their patience of delay,
their hope amid their pain,
their sacred zeal to burn away
disfigurement and stain;

5. Oh, by their fire of love, not less
in keenness than the flame;
oh, by their very helplessness,
oh, by thy own great name;

6. Good Jesus, help! sweet Jesus aid
the souls to thee most dear,
in prison for the debt unpaid
of sins committed here.

John Henry Newman (1801-90)

116

1. Here's a child for you, O Lord,
we shall cherish, we shall care.
We'll be faithful to your Word
for we want this child to share
your lovelight.

2. May he hold his head up high,
graceful, joyful, strong of limb.
May his eyes be clear and bright,
seeing beauty in all things
that you've made.

3. We were young ourselves, O Lord.
we were eager, we were fresh
like the opening buds of spring,
and we wanted happiness
in your way.

4. Then, at times, we went astray,
we were foolish, we were weak,
and the innocence we had
vanished like the trace of feet
when snow melts.

5. But we come, O Lord and king,
at your bidding, and we pray
that the precious gift we bring
will grow stronger every day
in your love.

6. By the water poured out here
and our promise, we believe,
he will master every fear,
and at last will come to see
your Godhead.

Estelle White

117

1. He's got the whole world
in his hand.
He's got the whole world
in his hand.
He's got the whole wide world
in his hand.
He's got the whole world
in his hand.

2. He's got you and me, brother . . .

3. He's got you and me, sister . . .

4. He's got everybody here . . .

5. He's got the whole world . . .

118   *Traditional*

1. He was born like you and I
in a body which must die,
yet his death was not for ever,
he lives on.
Who is this, like you and I
who was born to live and die,
yet his death was not for ever,
he lives on?

*Deep, deep, deep,
is the mystery I sing.
Dark, dark, dark is the riddle.
He was born like you and I
in a body which must die,
yet his death was not for ever:
he lives on.*

2. Not a soul, so it is said,
saw him raised up from the dead,
yet by now the story's known
throughout the world.
Who is this whom it is said
no one saw raised from the dead,
yet by now the story's known
throughout the world?

3. His believers, when they've met,
   know he's there with them, and yet
   he's with God (what makes us
       think that's somewhere else?)
   Who is this who, when they've met,
   is right there with them, and yet
   he's with God (what makes us
       think that's somewhere else?)

Hubert Richards

119

1. He who would valiant be
   'gainst all disaster,
   let him in constancy
   follow the master
   there's no discouragement
   shall make him once relent
   his first avowed intent
   to be a pilgrim.

2. Who so beset him round
   with dismal stories,
   do but themselves confound:
   his strength the more is.
   No foes shall stay his might
   though he with giants fight:
   he will make good his right
   to be a pilgrim.

3. Since, Lord, thou dost defend
   us with thy Spirit,
   we know we at the end
   shall life inherit.
   Then fancies flee away!
   I'll fear not what men say,
   I'll labour night and day
   to be a pilgrim.

Percy Dearmer (1867-1936),
after John Bunyan (1628-88)

120

1. Holy Father, God of might,
   throned amid the hosts of light,
   take our life, our strength, our love,
   King of earth and heaven above.

2. Hear the songs your people raise,
   songs of joyful thanks and praise,
   calling all created things
   to adore you, King of kings.

3. Christ, be with us as we go,
   let this blind world see and know,
   burning in our lives, the sight
   of its only saving light.

4. So, all men will bless your name,
   and your kingship all proclaim,
   praising with the heavenly host
   Father, Son and Holy Ghost.

Anonymous

121

1. Holy God, we praise thy name;
   Lord of all, we bow before thee!
   All on earth thy sceptre own,
   all in heaven above adore thee.
   Infinite thy vast domain,
   everlasting is thy reign.

2. Hark! the loud celestial hymn,
   angel choirs above are raising;
   cherubim and seraphim,
   in unceasing chorus praising,
   fill the heavens with sweet accord,
   holy, holy, holy Lord.

3. Holy Father, holy Son,
   Holy Spirit, three we name thee.
   While in essence only one.
   Undivided God we claim thee;
   and adoring bend the knee,
   while we own the mystery.

4. Spare thy people, Lord, we pray,
   by a thousand snares surrounded;
   keep us without sin to-day;
   never let us be confounded.
   Lo, I put my trust in thee,
   never, Lord, abandon me.

C. A. Walworth (1820-1900)

122

1. Holy, holy, holy, holy.
   Holy, holy, holy Lord
   God almighty.
   And we lift our hearts before you
   as a token of our love.
   Holy, holy, holy, holy.

2. Gracious Father, gracious Father,
   we are glad to be your children,
   gracious Father.
   And we lift our heads before you
   as a token of our love,
   gracious Father, gracious Father.

3. Precious Jesus, precious Jesus,
   we are glad you have redeemed us,
   precious Jesus.
   And we lift our hands before you
   as a token of our love,
   precious Jesus, precious Jesus.

4. Holy Spirit, Holy Spirit,
   come and fill our hearts anew,
   Holy Spirit.
   And we lift our voice before you
   as a token of our love,
   Holy Spirit, Holy Spirit.

5. Hallelujah, hallelujah,
   hallelujah, hallelujah,
   hallelujah.
   And we lift our hearts before you
   as a token of our love,
   hallelujah, hallelujah.

Jimmy Owens

123

1. Holy, holy, holy!
      Lord God almighty!
   Early in the morning
      our song shall rise to thee;
   holy, holy, holy!
      Merciful and mighty!
   God in three persons,
      blessed Trinity!

2. Holy, holy, holy!
      All the saints adore thee.
   Casting down their golden crowns
      around the glassy sea;
   Cherubim and seraphim
      falling down before thee,
   which wert, and art,
      and evermore shalt be.

3. Holy, holy, holy!
      Though the darkness hide thee,
   though the eye of sinful man
      thy glory may not see,
   only thou art holy,
      there is none beside thee,
   perfect in power,
      in love, and purity.

4. Holy, holy, holy!
      Lord God almighty!
   All thy works shall praise thy name,
      in earth, and sky, and sea;
   holy, holy, holy!
      Merciful and mighty!
   God in three persons,
      blessed Trinity!

Reginald Heber (1783-1875)

124

1. Holy Spirit, Lord of light,
   from the clear celestial height,
   thy pure beaming radiance give;
   come, thou Father of the poor,
   come with treasures which endure;
   come, thou light of all that live!

2. Thou, of all consolers best,
   thou, the soul's delightsome guest,
   dost refreshing peace bestow:
   thou in toil art comfort sweet;
   pleasant coolness in the heat;
   solace in the midst of woe.

3. Light immortal, light divine,
   visit thou these hearts of thine,
   and our inmost being fill:
   if thou take thy grace away,
   nothing pure in man will stay;
   all his good is turned to ill.

4. Heal our wounds, our strength
renew;
on our dryness pour thy dew;
wash the stains of guilt away:
Bend the stubborn heart and will;
melt the frozen, warm the chill;
guide the steps that go astray.

5. Thou, on those who evermore
thee confess and thee adore,
in thy sevenfold gifts descend:
Give them comfort when they die;
give them life with thee on high;
give them joys that never end.

Ascribed to Stephen Langton (d.1228)
tr. Edward Caswall

125

1. Holy Spirit of fire,
flame everlasting,
so bright and clear,
speak this day in our hearts.
Lighten our darkness
and purge us of fear,
Holy Spirit of fire.

The wind can blow or be still,
or water be parched by the sun.
A fire can die into dust:
but here the eternal Spirit of God
tells us a new world's begun.

2. Holy Spirit of love,
strong are the faithful
who trust your pow'r.
Love who conquer our will,
teach us the words of
the gospel of peace,
Holy Spirit of love.

3. Holy Spirit of God,
flame everlasting,
so bright and clear,
speak this day in our hearts.
Lighten our darkness
and purge us of fear,
Holy Spirit of God.

John Glynn

126

1. Holy Virgin, by God's decree,
you were called eternally;
that he could give
his Son to our race.
Mary, we praise you,
hail full of grace.

Ave, ave, ave, Maria.

2. By your faith and loving accord,
as the handmaid of the Lord,
you undertook
God's plan to embrace.
Mary, we thank you,
hail full of grace.

3. Refuge for your children so weak,
sure protection all can seek.
Problems of life
you help us to face.
Mary, we trust you,
hail full of grace.

4. To our needy world of today
love and beauty you portray,
showing the path
to Christ we must trace.
Mary, our mother,
hail, full of grace.

J-P. Lécot
tr. W. Raymond Lawrence

127

1. How dark was the stable
where Jesus was born?
How dark was the stable
that was his first home?
It was dark as the sky
on a black winter's night,
when the stars will not shine
and the moon gives no light.

2. How cold was the stable
where Jesus was born?
How cold was the stable
that was his first home?
It was cold as the frost
on a white window pane;
it was cold as a heart
that has known no love.

3. How light was the stable
      when Jesus was born?
   How light was the stable
      he made his first home?
   It was light as the star
      that was shining that night;
   it was light as an angel
      in splendour and might.

4. How warm was the stable
      when Jesus was born?
   How warm was the stable
      he made his first home?
   It was warm as the love
      of that first Christmas morn;
   it was warm as our hearts
      in which Jesus is born.

Michael Cockett

128

1. I am the bread of life.
   He who comes to me
      will never be hungry.
   I will raise him up.
      I will raise him up.
   I will raise him up to eternal life.
   I am the bread of life.

2. I am the spring of life.
   He who hopes in me
      will never be thirsty.
   I will raise him up.
      I will raise him up.
   I will raise him up to eternal life.
   I am the spring of life.

3. I am the way of life.
   He who follows me
      will never be lonely.
   I will raise him up.
      I will raise him up.
   I will raise him up to eternal life.
   I am the way of life.

4. I am the truth of life.
   He who looks for me
      will never seek blindly.
   I will raise him up.
      I will raise him up.
   I will raise him up to eternal life.
   I am the truth of life.

5. I am the life of life.
   He who dies with me
      will never die vainly.
   I will raise him up.
      I will raise him up.
   I will raise him up to eternal life.
   I am the life of life.

David Konstant

129

1. I believe in God almighty,
      who made heav'n and earth.
   I believe in one Lord,
      Jesus Christ, his only Son.
   God from God and Light from Light,
      the one truè God above,
   with the Father he is one
      creator of all things.

   Oh I believe in God almighty
      who made heav'n and earth.
   Yes, I believe in God almighty
      who made heav'n and earth.

2. For us all he came to earth and
      lived as one of us.
   For our sake he suffered death.
      They nailed him to a cross.
   But no earthly grave could hold the
      Lord of heav'n and earth;
   bursting forth he rose again,
      just as the prophets said.

3. Forty days he walked the earth,
      a dead man come alive.
   Then he bid his friends farewell,
      returning to his heav'n.
   He will come again to judge the
      living and the dead.
   He is Lord of all the worlds;
      his kingdom has no end.

4. I believe in God the Father,
      Spirit and the Son.
   I believe the Church is holy,
      universal, one.
   And through water all our guilt
      is cleansed   we are made new.
   Dying we will rise again
      to live for ever more.

Kevin Mayhew

130

1. I believe in God, the Father;
   I believe in God, his Son;
   I believe in God, their Spirit;
   each is God, yet God is one.

2. I believe what God has spoken
   through his Church, whose word is
        true;
   boldly she proclaims his Gospel,
   ever old, yet ever new.

3. All my hope is in God's goodness,
   shown for us by him who died,
   Jesus Christ, the world's Redeemer,
   spotless Victim crucified.

4. All my love is Love eternal;
   in that Love I love mankind.
   Take my heart, O Heart once broken,
   take my soul, my strength, my mind.

5. Father, I have sinned against you;
   look on me with eyes of love;
   seek your wand'ring sheep,
        Good Shepherd;
   grant heav'n's peace, O heav'nly Dove.

6. Bless'd be God, the loving Father;
   bless'd be God, his only Son;
   bless'd be God, all-holy Spirit;
   bless'd be God, for ever one.

James Quinn

131

1. I danced in the morning
   when the world was begun,
   and I danced in the moon
   and the stars and the sun,
   and I came down from heaven and
   I danced on the earth,
   at Bethlehem
   I had my birth.

   Dance, then, wherever you may be,
   I am the Lord of the Dance, said he.
   And I'll lead you all
        wherever you may be,
   and I'll lead you all
        in the dance, said he.

2. I danced for the scribe
   and the pharisee,
   but they would not dance
   and they wouldn't follow me.
   I danced for the fishermen,
   for James and John;
   they came with me
   and the dance went on.

3. I danced on the Sabbath
   and I cured the lame.
   The holy people they
   said it was a shame.
   They whipped and they stripped
   and they hung me on high,
   and they left me there
   on the cross to die.

4. I danced on a Friday
   when the sky turned black.
   It's hard to dance
   with the devil on your back.
   They buried my body
   and they thought I'd gone
   but I am the dance
   and I still go on.

5. They cut me down
   and I leapt up high.
   I am the life
   that'll never, never die.
   I'll live in you
   if you'll live in me.
   I am the Lord
   of the Dance, said he.

Sydney Carter

132

1. I'll sing a hymn to Mary,
   the Mother of my God,
   the Virgin of all virgins,
   of David's royal blood.
   O teach me, holy Mary,
   a loving song to frame,
   when wicked men blaspheme thee,
   to love and bless thy name.

2. O noble Tower of David,
   of gold and ivory,
   the Ark of God's own promise,
   the gate of heav'n to me,
   to live and not to love thee,
   would fill my soul with shame;
   when wicked men blaspheme thee,
   I'll love and bless thy name.

3. The Saints are high in glory,
   with golden crowns so bright;
   but brighter far is Mary,
   upon her throne of light.
   O that which God did give thee,
   let mortal ne'er disclaim;
   when wicked men blaspheme thee,
   I'll love and bless thy name.

4. But in the crown of Mary,
   there lies a wondrous gem,
   as Queen of all the Angels,
   which Mary shares with them:
   no sin hath e'er defiled thee,
   so doth our faith proclaim;
   when wicked men blaspheme thee,
   I'll love and bless thy name.

John Wyse (1825-98)

133

1. Immaculate Mary!
   Our hearts are on fire,
   that title so wondrous
   fills all our desire.

   Ave, ave, ave Maria!
   Ave, ave, ave Maria!

2. We pray for God's glory,
   may his kingdom come!
   We pray for his vicar,
   our father, and Rome.

3. We pray for our mother
   the church upon earth,
   and bless, sweetest Lady,
   the land of our birth.

4. O Mary! O mother!
   Reign o'er us once more,
   be England thy 'dowry'
   as in days of yore.

5. We pray for all sinners,
   and souls that now stray
   from Jesus and Mary,
   in heresy's way.

6. For poor, sick, afflicted
   thy mercy we crave;
   and comfort the dying
   thou light of the grave.

7. There is no need, Mary,
   nor ever has been,
   which thou canst not succour,
   Immaculate Queen.

8. In grief and temptation,
   in joy or in pain,
   we'll ask thee, our mother,
   nor seek thee in vain.

9. O bless us, dear Lady,
   with blessings from heaven.
   And to our petitions
   let answer be given.

10. In death's solemn moment,
    our mother, be nigh;
    as children of Mary
    O teach us to die.

11. And crown thy sweet mercy
    with this special grace,
    to behold soon in heaven
    God's ravishing face.

12. Now to God be all glory
    and worship for aye,
    and to God's virgin mother
    an endless Ave.

Anonymous

134

1. Immortal, invisible,
   God only wise.
   in light inaccessible
   hid from our eyes,
   most blessed, most glorious,
   the Ancient of Days,
   almighty, victorious,
   thy great name we praise.

2. Unresting, unhasting,
   and silent as light;
   nor wanting, nor wasting,
   thou rulest in might
   thy justice like mountains
   high-soaring above
   thy clouds which are fountains
   of goodness and love.

3. To all life thou givest,
   to both great and small;
   in all life thou livest,
   the true life of all;
   we blossom and flourish
   as leaves on the tree,
   and wither and perish;
   but naught changeth thee.

4. Great Father of glory,
   pure Father of light,
   thine angels adore thee,
   all veiling their sight;
   all laud we would render:
   O help us to see
   'tis only the splendour
   of light hideth thee.

W. Chalmers Smith (1825-1908)
Based on 1 Tim. 1: 17

135

1. In bread we bring you, Lord,
   our bodies' labour.
   In wine we offer you
   our spirits' grief.
   We do not ask you, Lord,
   who is my neighbour?
   But stand united now,
   one in belief.

Oh we have gladly heard
   your Word, your holy Word,
   and now in answer, Lord,
   our gifts we bring.
   Our selfish hearts make true,
   our failing faith renew,
   our lives belong to you,
   our Lord and King.

2. The bread we offer you
   is blessed and broken,
   and it becomes for us
   our spirits' food.
   Over the cup we bring
   your Word is spoken;
   make it your gift to us,
   your healing blood.
   Take all that daily toil
   plants in our heart's poor soil
   take all we start and spoil,
   each hopeful dream,
   the chances we have missed,
   the graces we resist,
   Lord, in thy Eucharist,
   take and redeem.

Kevin Nichols

136

1. In Christ there is no east or west,
   in him no south or north,
   but one great fellowship of love
   throughout the whole wide earth.

2. In him shall true hearts ev'rywhere
   their high communion find.
   His service is the golden cord
   close-binding all mankind.

3. Join hands, then, brothers of the
   faith
   whate'er your race may be.
   Who serves my Father as a son
   is surely kin to me.

4. In Christ now meet both east and
   west,
   in him meet south and north.
   All Christly souls are one in him
   throughout the whole wide earth.

John Oxenham (1852-1941)

137

1. In the bleak midwinter,
   frosty wind made moan,
   earth stood hard as iron,
   water like a stone;
   snow had fallen, snow on snow,
   snow on snow,
   in the bleak midwinter
   long ago.

2. Our God, heaven cannot hold him
   nor earth sustain;
   Heaven and earth shall flee away,
   when he comes to reign.
   In the bleak midwinter
   a stable-place sufficed
   the Lord God Almighty,
   Jesus Christ.

3. Enough for him, whom Cherubim
   worship night and day,
   a breastful of milk,
   and a mangerful of hay:
   enough for him, whom angels
   fall down before,
   the ox and ass and camel
   which adore.

4. Angels and archangels
   may have gathered there,
   Cherubim and Seraphim
   thronged the air.
   But only his mother
   in her maiden bliss
   worshipped the beloved
   with a kiss.

5. What can I give him,
   poor as I am?
   If I were a shepherd
   I would bring a lamb;
   if I were a wise man
   I would do my part;
   yet what I can I give him –
   give my heart.

   Christina G. Rossetti (1830-94)

138

1. In the earth the small seed
   is hidden and
   lies unseen until
   it is bidden by
   springtime stirrings up
   to the sunlight and
   summer ripening.
   Golden is the harvest
   and precious the
   bread that you are,
   and give to us, Lord.

2. In the vineyard branches
   are cut away
   so that fresh young shoots
   may, with ev'ry day,
   bend beneath the fruit
   as it ripens and
   fills with promise.
   Golden is the harvest
   and precious the
   wine that you are
   and give to us, Lord.

3. In me, Oh my Lord, plant
   the seed of love
   nourished by your body
   and by your blood.
   May my soul take wings
   and rise upwards to
   new awakenings!
   Golden is the light of
   your Godhead that
   by love you have,
   and give to us, Lord.

   Estelle White

139

1. Into one we all are gathered
    through the love of Christ.
   Let us then rejoice with gladness.
    In him we find love.
   Let us fear and love the living God,
   and love and cherish all mankind.

   Where charity and love are,
     there is God.

2. Therefore, when we are together
     in the love of Christ,
   let our minds know no division,
     strife or bitterness;
   may the Christ our God be in our
                              midst.
   Through Christ our Lord all love is
                              found.

3. May we see your face in glory,
     Christ our loving God.
   With the blessed saints of heaven
     give us lasting joy.
   We will then possess true happiness,
   and love for all eternity.

   Adapted from "Ubi Caritas et Amor"
                by Michael Cockett

140

1. I saw the grass, I saw the trees
   and the boats along the shore.
   I saw the shapes of many things
   I had only sensed before.
   And I saw the faces of men
     more clearly
   than if I had never been blind,
   the lines of envy around their lips
   and the greed
     and the hate in their eyes.
   And I turned away,
     yes, I turned away,
   for I had seen the perfect face
     of a real and proper man,
   the man who brought me
     from the dark
   into light, where life began.

2. I hurried then away from town
   to a quiet, lonely place.
   I found a clear, unruffled pool
   and I gazed upon my face.
   And I saw the image of me
     more clearly
   than if I had never been blind.
   The lines of envy around the lips
   and the greed
     and the hate in the eyes.
   And I turned away,
     yes, I turned away,
   for I had seen the perfect face
     of a real and proper man,
   the man who'd brought me
     from the dark
   into light, where life began.

3. I made my way into the town,
   to the busy, crowded streets,
   the shops and stalls and alley-ways,
   to the squalor and the heat.
   And I saw the faces of men
     more clearly
   than if I had never been blind,
   the lines of sorrow around their lips
   and the child
     looking out from their eyes,
   and I turned to them,
     yes, I turned to them,
   remembering the perfect face
     of a real and proper man,
   the man who'd brought me
     from the dark
   into light, where life began.

                        Estelle White

141

I sing a song to you, Lord,
a song of love and praise.
All glory be to you, Lord,
through everlasting days.

1. Holy, holy, holy,
   mighty Lord and God.
   He who was and is now,
   and who is to come.

2. Worthy is the slain Lamb,
   honour him and praise.
   We rejoice with gladness,
   sing our love today.

3. He has used his power,
   has begun his reign.
   So rejoice, you heavens,
   and proclaim his name.

4. Shine your light on us, Lord,
   let us know your way.
   Be our guide for ever,
   make us yours today.

142
Richard Beaumont

1. I sing the Lord God's praises,
   I answer to his call.
   His servant-girl he raises,
   she will be blessed by all.
   The Lord God gives his power
   to her who loves his name;
   o'er her his strength will tower,
   his mercies will remain.

2. Proud-hearted men he scatters,
   the strong will pass away;
   and for the kind and gentle
   there dawns the Lord's own day.
   Woe to the rich and mighty!
   He feeds and satisfies
   those who for justice hunger,
   and to him turn their eyes.

3. A Saviour he had promised
   to Abram long ago;
   and now to his own people
   his mercy he will show.
   Come let us praise our Father,
   for he fulfils his word,
   and sends his Holy Spirit
   through Jesus Christ our Lord.

143
W. F. Harwood

1. It came upon the midnight clear,
   that glorious song of old,
   from angels bending near the earth
   to touch their harps of gold;
   'Peace on the earth, good will to men,
   from heaven's all-gracious King!

The world in solemn stillness lay
to hear the angels sing.

2. Yet with the woes of sin and strife
   the world has suffered long;
   beneath the angel-strain have rolled
   two thousand years of wrong;
   and man, at war with man, hears not
   the love-song which they bring:
   O hush the noise, ye men of strife,
   and hear the angels sing!

3. For lo, the days are hastening on,
   by prophets seen of old,
   when with the ever-circling years
   shall come the time foretold,
   when the new heaven and earth
                              shall own
   the prince of peace their king,
   and all the world send back the song
   which now the angels sing.
   E. H. Sears (1810-76)

144

It's me, it's me, it's me, O Lord,
standin' in the need of pray'r.
It's me, it's me it's me, O Lord,
standin' in the need of pray'r.

1. Not my brother or my sister,
      but it's me, O Lord,
   standin' in the need of prayer.
   Not my brother or my sister,
      but it's me, O Lord,
   standin' in the need of pray'r.

2. Not my mother or my father,
      but it's me, O Lord,
   standin' in the need of prayer.
   Not my mother or my father,
      but it's me, O Lord,
   standin' in the need of pray'r.

3. Not the stranger or my neighbour,
      but it's me, O Lord,
   standin' in the need of prayer.
   Not the stranger or my neighbour,
      but it's me, O Lord,
   standin' in the need of pray'r.

Negro Spiritual

145

1. I watch the sunrise
   lighting the sky,
   casting its shadows near.
   And on this morning
   bright though it be,
   I feel those shadows near me.

   But you are always
   close to me
   following all my ways.
   May I be always
   close to you
   following all your ways, Lord.

2. I watch the sunlight
   shine through the clouds,
   warming the earth below.
   And at the mid-day
   life seems to say:
   "I feel your brightness near me."
   For you are always . . .

3. I watch the sunset
   fading away,
   lighting the clouds with sleep.
   And as the evening
   closes its eyes
   I feel your presence near me.
   For you are always . . .

4. I watch the moonlight
   guarding the night,
   waiting till morning comes.
   The air is silent,
   earth is at rest —
   only your peace is near me.
   Yes, you are always . . .

   John Glynn

146

1. I will give you glory,
   O God, my King.
   I will bless your name for ever.
   I will bless you day, after day.

   Day after day, after day, after day,
   after day, after day, after day.

2. I will sing your praises,
   O God, my King.
   I will bless your name for ever.
   I will bless you day, after day.

3. I will give you honour,
   O God, my King.
   I will bless your name for ever.
   I will bless you day, after day.

   Malcolm Campbell-Carr

147

1. I wonder as I wander
      out under the sky,
   how Jesus the Saviour
      did come for to die
   for poor ord'n'ry people
      like you and like I.
   I wonder as I wander
      out under the sky.

2. When Mary birthed Jesus,
      'twas in a cow's stall
   with wise men and farmers
      and shepherds and all.
   But high from God's heaven
      a star's light did fall,
   and the promise of ages
      it did then recall.

3. If Jesus had wanted
      for any wee thing,
   a star in the sky, or
      a bird on the wing,
   or all of God's angels
      in heav'n for to sing,
   he surely could have it,
      'cause he was the king.

   Traditional

148

1. January brings the snow,
   and the white frost glistens;
   I'm a child full of love,
   speak, Lord, and I'll listen.

2. March means sun and wind and rain,
   springtime flowers dancing.
   I am young, growing fast,
   wanting all the answers.

3. Maytime blossoms fill the air,
   here's a time for pleasure!
   Keep me safe, O my Lord,
   in my work and leisure.

4. In July the trees are tall,
   butterflies are roving.
   In my prime, may I be
   faithful in my loving.

5. In September's golden fields
   harvesters are reaping,
   and my mind gathers in
   mem'ries worth the keeping.

6. In November there are mists
   jewelling the grasses.
   Now my steps lose their spring;
   how each moment passes!

7. Come December days grow short
   and they say my life's through;
   but, my Lord, it's been good,
   and I want to thank you.

Estelle White

149

1. Jerusalem the golden,
   with milk and honey blest,
   beneath thy contemplation
   sink heart and voice oppressed.
   I know not, ah, I know not
   what joys await us there,
   what radiancy of glory,
   what bliss beyond compare.

2. They stand, those halls of Sion,
   all jubilant with song,
   and bright with many an angel,
   and all the martyr throng;
   the prince is ever in them,
   the daylight is serene;
   the pastures of the blessed
   are decked in glorious sheen.

3. There is the throne of David;
   and there, from care released,
   the shout of them that triumph,
   the song of them that feast;
   and they, who with their leader
   have conquered in the fight,
   for ever and for ever
   are clad in robes of white.

4. O sweet and blessed country,
   the home of God's elect!
   O sweet and blessed country
   that eager hearts expect!
   Jesus, in mercy bring us
   to that dear land of rest;
   who art, with God the Father
   and Spirit, ever blest.

From 'De Contemptu Mundi'
St. Bernard of Cluny, tr. J. M. Neale

150

1. Jesu, lover of my soul!
   Let me to thy bosom fly,
   while the nearer waters roll,
   while the tempest still is high;
   hide me, O my Saviour, hide,
   till the storm of life is past;
   safe into the haven guide,
   O receive my soul at last.

2. Other refuge have I none;
   hangs my helpless soul on thee;
   leave, ah! leave me not alone,
   still support and comfort me.
   All my trust on thee is stayed,
   all my help from thee I bring;
   cover my defenceless head
   with the shadow of thy wing.

3. Thou, O Christ, art all I want;
   more than all in thee I find;
   raise the fallen, cheer the faint,
   heal the sick and lead the blind,
   just and holy is thy name;
   I am all unrighteousness;
   false and full of sin I am,
   thou art full of truth and grace.

4. Plenteous grace with thee is found,
   grace to cover all my sin
   let the healing streams abound;
   make and keep me pure within.
   Thou of life the fountain art,
   freely let me take of thee;
   spring thou up within my heart,
   rise to all eternity.

   Charles Wesley (1707-88)

151

1. Jesu, meek and lowly,
   Saviour, pure and holy,
   on thy love relying,
   come I to thee flying.

2. Prince of life and power,
   my salvation's tower,
   on the cross I view thee,
   calling sinners to thee.

3. There behold me gazing
   at the sight amazing;
   bending low before thee,
   helpless I adore thee.

4. See the red wounds streaming,
   with Christ's life-blood gleaming,
   blood for sinners flowing,
   pardon free bestowing,

5. Fountains rich in blessing,
   Christ's fond love expressing,
   thou my aching sadness
   turnest into gladness.

6. Lord in mercy guide me,
   be thou e'er beside me,
   In thy ways direct me,
   'neath thy wings protect me.

   A. H. Collins (1827-1919)

152

1. Jesu, the very thought of thee
   with sweetness fills my breast;
   but sweeter far thy face to see,
   and in thy presence rest.

2. Nor voice can sing, nor heart can
                             frame,
   nor can the memory find,
   a sweeter sound than thy blest name,
   O Saviour of mankind.

3. O hope of every contrite heart,
   O joy of all the meek,
   to those who fall, how kind thou art,
   how good to those who seek!

4. But what to those who find? Ah, this
   nor tongue nor pen can show;
   the love of Jesus, what it is
   none but his lovers know.

5. Jesu, our only joy be thou,
   as thou our prize wilt be;
   Jesu, be thou our glory now,
   and through eternity.

   11th c.,tr. Edward Caswall

153

1. Jesus Christ is risen today,
      alleluia!
   Our triumphant holy day,
      alleluia!
   Who did once, upon the cross,
      alleluia!
   Suffer to redeem our loss,
      alleluia!

2. Hymns of praise then let us sing,
      alleluia!
   Unto Christ, our heavenly king,
      alleluia!
   Who endured the cross and grave,
      alleluia!
   Sinners to redeem and save,
      alleluia!

3. But the pains that he endured,
      alleluia!
   Our salvation have procured;
      alleluia!

Now above the sky he's king,
alleluia!
Where the angels ever sing,
alleluia!

Lyra Davidica (1708) and the
Supplement (1816).
Based partly on 'Surrexit Christus
hodie. (14th c.)

154

1. Jesus, gentlest Saviour,
   God of might and power,
   thou thyself art dwelling
   in us at this hour.
   Nature cannot hold thee,
   heav'n is all too strait
   for thine endless glory,
   and thy royal state.

2. Yet the hearts of children,
   hold what worlds cannot,
   and the God of wonders
   loves the lowly spot.
   Jesus, gentlest Saviour,
   thou art in us now,
   fill us full of goodness,
   till our hearts o'erflow.

3. Pray the prayer within us
   that to heaven shall rise;
   sing the song that angels
   sing above the skies;
   multiply our graces,
   chiefly love and fear;
   and, dear Lord, the chiefest,
   grace to persevere.

   Frederick William Faber (1814-63)

155

1. Jesus, Lord, I'll sing a song
   that's soft and low for you,
   so you can join with me
   and sing it too.
   You have said that when we pray,
   then you are praying too,
   and when your Father hears us,
   he hears you.

Our Father who art in heaven,
hallowed be thy name,
hallowed be thy name.

2. I believe that you are here
   with me and praying too.
   Your Father loves me
   because I love you.
   Jesus, Lord, I'll sing a song that's
   soft and low for you,
   so you can join with me
   and sing it too.

   Briege O'Hare

156

1. Jesus is God! The solid earth,
   the ocean broad and bright,
   the countless stars, the golden dust,
   that strew the skies at night,
   the wheeling storm, the dreadful
   fire,
   the pleasant wholesome air,
   the summer's sun, the winter's frost,
   his own creations were.

2. Jesus is God! the glorious bands
   of golden angels sing
   songs of adoring praise to him,
   their maker and their king.
   He was true God in Bethlehem's
   crib,
   on Calvary's cross true God,
   he who in heaven eternal reigned,
   in time on earth abode.

3. Jesus is God! Let sorrow come,
   and pain and every ill;
   all are worth while, for all are means
   his glory to fulfil;
   worth while a thousand years of life
   to speak one little word,
   if by our Credo we might own
   the Godhead of our Lord.

   Frederick William Faber (1814-63)

157

1. Jesus, my Lord, my God, my all,
   how can I love thee as I ought?
   And how revere this wondrous gift
   so far surpassing hope or thought?

   Sweet Sacrament, we thee adore;
   Oh, make us love thee more and
   more.

2. Had I but Mary's sinless heart
   to love thee with, my dearest King,
   Oh, with what bursts of fervent
                                   praise
   thy goodness, Jesus, would I sing!

3. Ah, see! within a creature's hand
   the vast Creator deigns to be,
   reposing, infant-like, as though
   on Joseph's arm, or Mary's knee.

4. Thy body, soul, and Godhead, all;
   O mystery of love divine!
   I cannot compass all I have,
   for all thou hast and art are mine;

5. Sound, sound, his praises higher
                                   still,
   and come, ye angels, to our aid;
   'tis God, 'tis God, the very God
   whose power both man and angels
                                   made.

   Frederick William Faber (1814-63)

158

1. Jesus! thou art coming,
   holy as thou art,
   thou, the God who made me,
   to my sinful heart.
   Jesus! I believe it,
   on thy only word;
   kneeling, I adore thee,
   as my king and Lord.

2. Who am I, my Jesus,
   that thou com'st to me?
   I have sinned against thee,
   often grievously;
   I am very sorry
   I have caused thee pain.
   I will never, never,
   wound thy heart again.

3. Put thy kind arms round me,
   feeble as I am;
   thou art my Good Shepherd,
   I, thy little lamb;
   since thou comest, Jesus,
   now to be my guest,
   I can trust thee always,
   Lord, for all the rest.

4. Dearest Lord, I love thee,
   with my whole heart,
   not for what thou givest,
   but for what thou art.
   Come, oh, come, sweet Saviour!
   Come to me, and stay,
   for I want thee, Jesus,
   more than I can say.

5. Ah! what gift or present,
   Jesus, can I bring?
   I have nothing worthy
   of my God and King;
   but thou art my shepherd:
   I, thy little lamb,
   take myself, dear Jesus,
   all I have and am.

6. Take my body, Jesus,
   eyes, and ears and tongue;
   never let them, Jesus,
   help to do thee wrong.
   Take my heart, and fill it
   full of love for thee;
   all I have I give thee,
   give thyself to me.

   S.N.D

159

1. Just a closer walk with thee,
   grant it, Jesus if you please;
   daily walking close to thee,
   let it be, dear Lord, let it be.

2. Through the day of toil that's near,
   if I fall, dear Lord, who cares.
   Who with me my burden share?
   None but thee, dear Lord, none but
                                    thee.

3. When my feeble life is o'er,
   time for me will be no more.
   Guide me gently, safely on
   to the shore, dear Lord, to the
                                  shore.

Traditional

160

1. Keep we the fast that men of old
   learned from on high in mystic
                                 ways,
   till yonder sun hath duly told
   his hallowed tale of forty days.

2. This covenant, long since revealed
   to patriarchs and ardent seers,
   Christ by his own example sealed,
   author of time, and Lord of years.

3. More wisely therefore let us walk,
   sparing of food and wine and sleep;
   over our trifles and our talk
   more jealous be the watch we keep.

4. Still by our sins, O Lord, we grieve
   thy love, so full of pardon free:
   author of mercy, still reprieve
   the souls that turn again to thee.

5. Remember whence our fashion
                              came,
   frail creatures, yet thy creatures still,
   crush, for the glory of thy name,
   the murm'rings of our stubborn will.

6. The guilt that dooms us put away,
   with larger grace our prayers
                              requite,
   at last, and ever from this day,
   teach us to live as in thy sight.

7. Hear us, O Trinity sublime,
   and undivided unity;
   so let this consecrated time
   bring forth thy fruits abundantly.

St. Gregory the Great (540-604)
tr. R. A. Knox

161

1. King of glory, king of peace,
   I will love thee;
   and that love may never cease,
   I will move thee.
   Thou hast granted my request,
   thou hast heard me;
   thou didst note my working breast,
   thou hast spared me.

2. Wherefore with my utmost art,
   I will sing thee.
   And the cream of all my heart
   I will bring thee,
   though my sins against me cried,
   thou didst clear me;
   and alone, when they replied,
   thou didst hear me.

3. Seven whole days, not one in seven,
   I will praise thee;
   in my heart, though not in heaven,
   I can raise thee.
   Small it is, in this poor sort
   to enrol thee:
   e'en eternity's too short
   to extol thee.

George Herbert (1593-1633)

162

1. Kum ba yah, my Lord,
    kum ba yah,
    kum ba yah, my Lord,
    kum ba yah!
    Kum ba yah, my Lord,
    kum ba yah!
    O Lord, kum ba yah.

2. Someone's crying, Lord,
    kum ba yah,
    someone's crying, Lord,
    kum ba yah!
    Someone's crying, Lord,
    kum ba yah!
    O Lord, kum ba yah.

3. Someone's singing, Lord,
    kum ba yah,
    someone's singing, Lord,
    kum ba yah!
    Someone's singing, Lord,
    kum ba yah!
    O Lord, kum ba yah.

4. Someone's praying, Lord,
    kum ba yah,
    someone's praying, Lord,
    kum ba yah!
    Someone's praying, Lord,
    kum ba yah!
    O Lord, kum ba yah.

Spiritual

163

1. Leader now on earth no longer,
    soldier of th'eternal king,
    victor in the fight for heaven,
    we thy loving praises sing.

    Great Saint George,
    our patron, help us,
    in the conflict be thou nigh;
    help us in that daily battle,
    where each one must win or die.

2. Praise him who in deadly battle
    never shrank from foeman's sword,
    proof against all earthly weapon,
    gave his life for Christ the Lord.

3. Who, when earthly war was over,
    fought, but not for earth's renown;
    fought, and won a nobler glory,
    won the martyr's purple crown.

4. Help us when temptation presses,
    we have still our crown to win,
    help us when our soul is weary
    fighting with the powers of sin.

5. Clothe us in thy shining armour,
    place thy good sword in our hand;
    teach us how to wield it, fighting
    onward towards the heavenly land.

6. Onward, till, our striving over,
    on life's battlefield we fall,
    resting then, but ever ready,
    waiting for the angel's call.

Joseph W. Reeks (1849-1900)

164

1. Lead, kindly light
        amid th'encircling gloom,
    lead thou me on;
    the night is dark,
        and I am far from home,
    lead thou me on.
    Keep thou my feet;
        I do not ask to see
    the distant scene;
        one step enough for me.

2. I was not ever thus,
        nor prayed that thou
    shouldst lead me on;
    I loved to choose
        and see my path; but now
    lead thou me on.
    I loved the garish day,
        and, spite of fears,
    pride ruled my will;
        remember not past years.

3. So long thy power
    hath blest me, sure it still
    will lead me on
    o'er moor and fen,
       o'er crag and torrent, till
    the night is gone,
    and with the morn
       those angel faces smile
    which I have loved
    long since, and lost awhile.

John Henry Newman (1801-90)

165

1. Lead us, heav'nly Father, lead us
    o'er the world's tempestuous sea;
    guard us, guide us, keep us, feed us,
    for we have no help but thee;
    yet possessing ev'ry blessing
    if our God our Father be.

2. Saviour, breathe forgiveness o'er us,
    all our weakness thou dost know,
    thou didst tread this earth before us,
    thou didst feel its keenest woe;
    lone and dreary, faint and weary,
    through the desert thou didst go.

3. Spirit of our God, descending,
    fill our hearts with heavenly joy,
    love with every passion blending,
    pleasure that can never cloy;
    thus provided, pardoned, guided,
    nothing can our peace destroy.

J. Edmeston (1791-1867)

166

1. Let all mortal flesh keep silence
    and with fear and trembling stand,
    ponder nothing earthly-minded:
    for with blessing in his hand,
    Christ our God on earth descendeth,
    our full homage to demand.

2. King of kings, yet born of Mary,
    as of old on earth he stood
    Lord of lords, in human vesture –
    in the Body and the Blood.
    He will give to all the faithful
    his own Self for heavenly Food.

3. Rank on rank the host of heaven
    spreads its vanguard on the way,
    as the Light of Light descendeth
    from the realms of endless day,
    that the powers of hell may vanish
    as the darkness clears away.

4. At his feet the six-winged Seraph;
    Cherubim with sleepless eye,
    veil their faces to the Presence,
    as with ceaseless voice they cry,
    alleluia, alleluia,
    alleluia, Lord most high.

Liturgy of St. James, tr. G. Moultrie

167

1. Let all that is within me cry holy.
    Let all that is within me cry holy.
    Holy, holy, holy
       is the Lamb that was slain.

2. Let all that is within me cry mighty.
    Let all that is within me cry mighty.
    Mighty, mighty, mighty
       is the Lamb that was slain.

3. Let all that is within me cry worthy.
    Let all that is within me cry worthy.
    Worthy, worthy, worthy
       is the Lamb that was slain.

4. Let all that is within me cry blessed.
    Let all that is within me cry blessed.
    Blessed, blessed, blessed
       is the Lamb that was slain.

5. Let all that is within me cry Jesus.
    Let all that is within me cry Jesus.
    Jesus, Jesus, Jesus
       is the Lamb that was slain.

Traditional

168

1. Let all the world
   in every corner sing,
   my God and King!
   The heav'ns are not too high,
   his praise may thither fly;
   the earth is not too low,
   his praises there may grow.
   Let all the world
   in every corner sing,
   my God and King!

2. Let all the world
   in every corner sing,
   my God and King!
   The church with psalms must shout,
   no door can keep them out;
   but, above all, the heart
   must bear the longest part.
   Let all the world
   in every corner sing,
   my God and King!

George Herbert (1593-1633)

169

1. Let us break bread together
   on our knees.
   Let us break bread together
   on our knees.
   When I fall on my knees
   with my face to the rising sun,
   Oh Lord, have mercy on me.

2. Let us drink wine together . . .

3. Let us praise God together . . .

Traditional

170

1. Let's make peace in our hearts.
   Let's make peace in our hearts.
   Let's make true peace in our hearts.
   Let's make true peace in our hearts.

2. Let's take peace into the world.
   Let's take peace into the world.
   Let's take true peace into the world.
   Let's take true peace into the world.

3. Let's share peace with ev'ryone.
   Let's share peace with ev'ryone.
   Let's share true peace with ev'ryone.
   Let's share true peace with ev'ryone.

4. My peace I leave with you.
   My peace I give to you.
   Not as the world gives do I give,
   but true peace I give unto you.

Sebastian Temple

171

1. Let us, with a gladsome mind,
   praise the Lord, for he is kind;

   *For his mercies aye endure,
   ever faithful, ever sure.*

2. Let us blaze his name abroad,
   for of gods he is the God;

3. He, with all-commanding might,
   filled the new-made world with
   light;

4. He the golden-tressed sun
   caused all day his course to run:

5. And the horned moon at night,
   'mid her spangled sisters bright:

6. All things living he doth feed,
   his full hand supplies their need:

7. Let us, with a gladsome mind,
   praise the Lord, for he is kind.

*John Milton (1608-75),
based on Ps. 136*

172

1. Light of our darkness, Word of God,
   sent to illumine our earthly night,
   you we salute with singing hearts,
   bathed in the splendour of your
   light.

2. Sword that can pierce the inmost
   soul,
   stripping whatever thoughts are
   there,
   cut to the marrow of our minds,
   enter our hearts and lay them bare.

3. Vessel of God's abundant life,
   bearer of truth that sets us free,
   breaking the deadly grasp of sin,
   work in our hearts your mystery.

4. Word that has overcome the world,
   seed of immortal destiny,
   grow in our hearts, that we may live
   sharing your deathless victory.

Richard Connolly

173

1. Little flower in the ground,
   petals falling all around.
   Summer's past and Autumn's here
   and now we know your end is near.

2. Seeds that fall on to the ground
   by the winds are scattered round.
   Some will feed the Winter birds,
   and some will nestle in the earth.

3. Some will last the Winter through
   'till the Spring makes all things new.
   See the flower newly grown
   from seeds the Winter wind has
   sown.

4. Praise the Lord in heav'n above,
   who shows us all the way of love.
   Praise him for the dying year.
   If Winter comes then Spring is near.

Michael Cockett

174

1. Little Jesus, sweetly sleep,
   do not stir;
   we will lend a coat of fur,
   we will rock you,
   rock you, rock you,
   we will rock you,
   rock you, rock you,
   see the fur to keep you warm
   snugly round your tiny form.

2. Mary's little baby sleep,
   sweetly sleep,
   sleep in comfort, slumber deep;
   we will rock you,
   rock you, rock you,
   we will rock you,
   rock you, rock you,
   we will serve you all we can,
   darling, darling little man.

Czech., tr. O.B.C.

175

1. Long ago in Bethlehem,
   you were lying in a manger
   in the midst of human danger,
   at your mother's knee.
   Hosanna, alleluia,
   hosanna, alleluia,
   hosanna, alleluia,
   at your mother's knee.

2. Now as King we hail the baby,
   living faith proclaims the story
   of that humble manger glory,
   stabled in the hay.
   Hosanna, alleluia,
   hosanna, alleluia,
   hosanna, alleluia,
   Christ is King today.

Ian Sharp

176

1. Look down, O Mother Mary,
from thy bright throne above;
cast down upon thy children
one only glance of love;
and if a heart so tender
with pity flows not o'er,
then turn away, O Mother,
and look on us no more.

Look down O Mother Mary,
from thy bright throne above,
cast down upon thy children,
one only glance of love.

2. See how, ungrateful sinners,
we stand before thy Son;
his loving heart upbraids us
the evil we have done,
but if thou wilt appease him,
speak for us but one word;
for thus thou canst obtain us,
the pardon of Our Lord.

3. O Mary, dearest Mother,
if thou wouldst have us live,
say that we are thy children,
and Jesus will forgive.
Our sins make us unworthy
that title still to bear,
but thou art still our mother;
then show a mother's care.

4. Unfold to us thy mantle,
there stay we without fear;
what evil can befall us
if, mother, thou art near?
O kindest, dearest mother
thy sinful children save;
look down on us with pity,
who thy protection crave.

St. Alphonsus (1696-1787),
tr. Edmund Vaughan

177

1. Lord accept the gifts we offer
at this Eucharistic feast,
bread and wine to be transformed
now
through the action of thy priest
take us too, Lord, and transform us,
be thy grace in us increased.

2. May our souls be pure and spotless
as the host of wheat so fine;
may all stain of sin be crushed out,
like the grape that forms the wine,
as we, too, become partakers,
in this sacrifice divine.

3. Take our gifts, almighty Father,
living God, eternal, true,
which we give through Christ, our
Saviour,
pleading here for us anew
grant salvation to all present,
and our faith and love renew.

Sister M. Teresine

178

1. Lord, for tomorrow and its needs
I do not pray;
keep me, my God, from stain of sin,
just for today.

2. Let me both diligently work
and duly pray;
let me be kind in word and deed,
just for today.

3. Let me be slow to do my will,
prompt to obey;
help me to mortify my flesh,
just for today.

4. Let me no wrong or idle word
unthinking say;
set thou a seal upon my lips,
just for today.

5. Let me in season, Lord, be grave,
in season, gay;
let me be faithful to thy grace,
just for today.

6. And if today my tide of life
should ebb away,
give me thy sacraments divine,
sweet Lord, today.

7. So, for tomorrow and its needs
I do not pray;
but keep me, guide me, love me,
Lord,
just for today.

Sister M. Xavier

179

1. Lord, Jesus Christ,
   you have come to us
   you are one with us, Mary's son.
   Cleansing our souls from all their sin,
   pouring your love and goodness in,
   Jesus our love for you we sing,
   living Lord.

2. Lord Jesus Christ,
   now and ev'ry day
   teach us how to pray, Son of God.
   You have commanded us to do
   this in remembrance, Lord, of you
   Into our lives your pow'r breaks
                  through,
   living Lord.

3. Lord Jesus Christ,
   you have come to us,
   born as one of us, Mary's Son.
   Led out to die on Calvary,
   risen from death to set us free,
   living Lord Jesus, help us see
   you are Lord.

4. Lord Jesus Christ,
   I would come to you,
   live my life for you, Son of God.
   All your commands I know are true,
   your many gifts will make me new,
   into my life your pow'r breaks
                  through,
   living Lord.

Patrick Appleford

180

1. Lord Jesus, think on me,
   and purge away my sin;
   from earthborn passions set me free,
   and make me pure within.

2. Lord Jesus, think on me,
   with care and woe oppressed;
   let me thy loving servant be,
   and taste thy promised rest.

3. Lord Jesus, think on me
   amid the battle's strife;
   in all my pain and misery
   be thou my health and life.

4. Lord Jesus, think on me,
   nor let me go astray;
   through darkness and perplexity
   point thou the heavenly way.

5. Lord Jesus, think on me,
   when flows the tempest high:
   when on doth rush the enemy,
   O Saviour, be thou nigh.

6. Lord Jesus, think on me,
   that, when the flood is past,
   I may the eternal brightness see,
   and share thy joy at last.

*Bishop Synesius (375-43
tr. A. W. Chatfie*

181

1. Lord of all hopefulness,
   Lord of all joy,
   whose trust, ever child-like,
   no cares could destroy,
   be there at our waking,
   and give us, we pray,
   your bliss in our hearts, Lord,
   at the break of the day.

2. Lord of all eagerness,
   Lord of all faith,
   whose strong hands were skilled
   at the plane and the lathe,
   be there at our labours,
   and give us, we pray,
   your strength in our hearts, Lord,
   at the noon of the day.

3. Lord, of all kindliness,
   Lord of all grace,
   your hands swift to welcome,
   your arms to embrace,
   be there at our homing,
   and give us, we pray,
   your love in our hearts, Lord,
   at the eve of the day.

4. Lord of all gentleness,
   Lord of all calm,
   whose voice is contentment,
   whose presence is balm,
   be there at our sleeping,
   and give us, we pray,
   your peace in our hearts, Lord,
   at the end of the day.

   Jan Struther (1901-53)

182

1. Lord, we pray for golden peace,
   peace all over the land,
   may all men dwell in liberty,
   all walking hand in hand.

   Banish fear and ignorance,
   hunger, thirst and pain.
   Banish hate and poverty,
   let no man live in vain,
   let no man live in vain.

2. Keep all men for ever one,
   one in love and in grace.
   And wipe away all war and strife,
   give freedom to each race.

3. Let your justice reign supreme.
   Righteousness always done.
   Let goodness rule the hearts of men
   and evil overcome.

   Sebastian Temple

183

1. Lord, who throughout these forty
                                days
   for us didst fast and pray,
   teach us with thee to mourn our sins,
   and at thy side to stay.

2. As thou with Satan didst contend,
   and didst the victory win,
   O give us strength in thee to fight,
   in thee to conquer sin.

3. As thirst and hunger thou didst bear,
   so teach us, gracious Lord,
   to die to self, and daily live
   by thy most holy word.

4. And through these days of
                           penitence,
   and through thy Passiontide,
   yea, evermore, in life and death,
   Lord Christ, with us abide.

   Claudia Frances Hernaman (1838-98)

184

1. Love divine, all loves excelling,
   joy of heaven, to earth come down,
   fix in us thy humble dwelling,
   all thy faithful mercies crown.

2. Jesus, thou art all compassion,
   pure unbounded love thou art;
   visit us with thy salvation,
   enter every trembling heart.

3. Come, almighty to deliver,
   let us all thy life receive;
   suddenly return, and never,
   never more thy temples leave.

4. Thee we would be always blessing,
   serve thee as thy hosts above;
   pray, and praise thee without
                              ceasing,
   glory in thy perfect love.

5. Finish then thy new creation,
   pure and sinless let us be;
   let us see thy great salvation
   perfectly restored in thee.

6. Changed from glory into glory,
   till in heaven we take our place,
   till we cast our crowns before thee,
   lost in wonder, love, and praise.

   Charles Wesley (1707-88)

185

1. Love is his word, love is his way,
   feasting with men, fasting alone,
   living and dying, rising again,
   love, only love, is his way.

   Richer than gold
   is the love of my Lord:
   better than splendour and wealth.

2. Love is his way, love is his mark,
   sharing his last Passover feast,
   Christ at his table, host to the
   Twelve,
   love, only love, is his mark.

3. Love is his mark, love is his sign,
   bread for our strength, wine for our
   joy,
   "This is my body, this is my blood,"
   love, only love, is his sign.

4. Love is his sign, love is his news,
   "Do this," he said, "lest you forget
   all my deep sorrow, all my dear
   blood,"
   love, only love, is his news.

5. Love is his news, love is his name,
   we are his own, chosen and called,
   family, brethren, cousins and kin.
   Love, only love, is his name.

6. Love is his name, love is his law.
   Hear his command, all who are his·
   "Love one another, I have loved
   you."
   Love, only love, is his law.

7. Love is his law, love is his word:
   love of the Lord, Father and Word,
   love of the Spirit, God ever one,
   love, only love, is his word.

   Luke Connaughton

186

1. Loving Father, from thy bounty
   choicest gifts unnumbered flow:
   all the blessings of salvation,
   which to Christ thy Son we owe,
   all the gifts that by thy bidding
   nature's hands on us bestow!

2. Here thy grateful children gather,
   offering gifts of bread and wine;
   these we give to thee in homage,
   of our love the loving sign,
   and restore to thee creation,
   given to man, yet ever thine!

3. Soon will come Christ's loving
   presence,
   on our love to set his seal!
   Body broken, Blood shed for us,
   bread and wine will then reveal!
   bread and wine, though these no
   longer,
   flesh and blood will yet conceal!

   James Quinn, S.J.

187

1. Loving shepherd of thy sheep,
   keep me, Lord, in safety keep;
   nothing can thy pow'r withstand,
   none can pluck me from thy hand.

2. Loving shepherd, thou didst give
   thine own life that I might live;
   may I love thee day by day,
   gladly thy sweet will obey.

3. Loving shepherd, ever near,
   teach me still thy voice to hear;
   suffer not my steps to stray
   from the strait and narrow way.

4. Where thou leadest may I go,
   walking in thy steps below;
   then before thy Father's throne,
   Jesu, claim me for thine own.

   Jane E. Leeson (1807-82)

188

1. Maiden, yet a mother,
   daughter of thy Son,
   high beyond all other,
   lowlier is none;
   thou the consummation
   planned by God's decree,
   when our lost creation
   nobler rose in thee!

2. Thus his place prepared,
   he who all things made
   'mid his creatures tarried,
   in thy bosom laid;
   there his love he nourished,
   warmth that gave increase
   to the root whence flourished
   our eternal peace.

3. Noon on Sion's mountain
   is thy charity;
   hope its living fountain
   finds, on earth, in thee:
   lady, such thy power,
   he, who grace would buy
   not as of thy dower,
   without wings would fly.

   Dante Alighieri (1265-1321)
   tr. R. A. Knox

189

1. Make me a channel of your peace.
   Where there is hatred,
      let me bring your love.
   Where there is injury,
      your pardon, Lord.
   And where there's doubt,
      true faith in you.

2. Make me a channel of your peace.
   Where there's despair in life,
      let me bring hope.
   Where there is darkness
      only light,
   and where there's sadness
      ever joy.

3. Oh, Master,
      grant that I may never seek
   so much to be consoled
      as to console,
   to be understood as to understand,
   to be loved, as to love,
      with all my soul.

4. Make a channel of your peace.
   It is in pardoning
      that we are pardoned,
   in giving to all men
      that we receive,
   and in dying that we're
      born to eternal life.

   Sebastian Temple

190

1. Man of Galilee
   will you come and stand by me
   through the length of each working
                              day?
   Bless, O Lord, my efforts, I pray.

2. Man who healed the blind
   open up the eyes of my mind
   to the needs of my fellow man.
   Help me give with open hands.

3. Man of bread and of wine
   show me by the means of this sign
   that I share your life and your light
   with the neighbour here at my side.

4. Man of Calvary
   give me strength and will to be free
   of the weight of self-pity's chains,
   then my trials will be but gains.

5. Man at God's right hand,
   will you help me understand
   that in you, when my breath is
                              stilled,
   all my longings will be fulfilled?

   Estelle White

191

1. Many times I have turned
     from the way of the Lord,
   many times
     I have chosen the darkness.
   In the light of the day,
     when the shadows are gone,
   all I see is my sin
     in its starkness.

   Jesus came to bring us mercy.
   Jesus came to bring us life again.
   He loves us, he loves us, he loves us!

2. I confess I have sinned
     in the sight of the Lord,
   through my pride,
     through my malice and weakness.
   I've rejected the promise
     that comes from the cross
   where the Lord hung above
     us in meakness.

3. With a word, with a deed,
     with a failure to act,
   with a thought
     that was evil and hateful,
   I confess to you,
     brothers and sisters of mine,
   I have sinned and
     been proven ungrateful.

4. Through my fault, through my fault,
     through my serious fault,
   I confess to you,
     Lord, all my sinning.
   But look down on me, Lord,
     grant your pardon and peace;
   with your help, I've a
     new life beginning.

   Willard F. Jabusch

192

1. Mary immaculate,
     star of the morning,
   chosen before
     the creation began,
   chosen to bring,
     for thy bridal adorning,
   woe to the serpent
     and rescue to man.

2. Here, in an orbit
     of shadow and sadness
   veiling thy splendour,
     thy course thou hast run;
   now thou art throned in all glory
     and gladness,
   crowned by the hand
     of thy saviour and Son.

3. Sinners, we worship
     thy sinless perfection,
   fallen and weak,
     for thy pity we plead;
   grant us the shield
     of thy sovereign protection,
   measure thine aid
     by the depth of our need.

4. Frail is our nature,
     and strict our probation,
   watchful the foe
     that would lure us to wrong,
   succour our souls
     in the hour of temptation,
   Mary immaculate
     tender and strong.

5. See how the wiles
     of the serpent assail us,
   see how we waver
     and flinch in the fight;
   let thine immaculate
     merit avail us,
   make of our weakness
     a proof of thy might.

6. Bend from thy throne
     at the voice of our crying;
   bend to this earth
     which thy footsteps have trod;
   stretch out thine arms
     to us living and dying,
   Mary immaculate,
     mother of God.

   F. W. Weatherell

193

May the peace of Christ
  be with you today,
may the peace of Christ
  be with you today,
may the love of Christ,
the joy of Christ,
may the peace of Christ be yours.

Kevin Mayhew

194

1. Merrily on, merrily on
  flow the bright waters
    that carry a song,
  a song that is sung
    of the love of the Lord,
  a love that is endless
    and ever outpoured.

2. Father above, Father above,
  source of our life and
    our strength and our love,
  as fresh as the spring
    that is limpid and clear,
  your presence is young
    and will always be near.

3. Son from on high, Son from on high,
  you who united
    the earth and the sky,
  Oh, cleanse us with water
    and fill us with peace,
  our river of mercy
    who never will cease.

4. Spirit of God, Spirit of God,
  breathe on the waters
    and flow in the flood,
  and open the flood-gates
    that lead to the sea
    — the ocean is open
    and boundless and free!

5. Merrily on, merrily on
  flow the bright waters
    that carry a song,
  a song that is sung
    of the love of the Lord,
  a love that is endless
    and ever outpoured.

John Glynn

195

1. Mine eyes have seen the glory
  of the coming of the Lord.
He is trampling out the vintage
  where the grapes of wrath are stored.
He has loosed the fateful lightning
  of his terrible swift sword.
His truth is marching on.

Glory, glory halleluja!
Glory, glory halleluja!
Glory, glory halleluja!
His truth is marching on.

2. I have seen him in the watchfires
  of a hundred circling camps.
They have gilded him an altar
  in the evening dews and damps.
I can read his righteous sentence
  by the dim and flaring lamps.
His day is marching on.

3. He has sounded forth the trumpet
  that shall never sound retreat.
He is sifting out the hearts of men
  before his judgement seat.
O, be swift my soul to answer him,
  be jubilant my feet!
Our God is marching on.

4. In the beauty of the lilies
  Christ was born across the sea
with a glory in his bosom
  that transfigures you and me.
As he died to make men holy,
  let us die to make men free.
Whilst God is marching on.

Julia Ward Howe (1819-1910)

196

1. Morning has broken
   like the first morning,
   blackbird has spoken
   like the first bird.
   Praise for the singing!
   Praise for the morning!
   Praise for them, springing
   fresh from the Word!

2. Sweet the rain's new fall
   sunlit from heaven,
   like the first dew-fall
   on the first grass.
   Praise for the sweetness
   of the wet garden,
   sprung in completeness
   where his feet pass.

3. Mine is the sunlight!
   Mine is the morning
   born of the one light
   Eden saw play!
   Praise with elation,
   praise ev'ry morning,
   God's re-creation
   of the new day!

   Eleanor Farjeon (1881-1965)

197

1. "Moses I know you're the man,"
   the Lord said.
   "You're going to work out my
       plan,"
   the Lord said.
   "Lead all the Israelites
       out of slavery."
   And I shall make them a
       wandering race
   called the people of God."

   So ev'ry day we're on our way,
   for we're a travelling,
       wandering race
   called the people of God.

2. "Don't get too set in your ways,"
   the Lord said.
   "Each step is only a phase,"
   the Lord said.
   "I'll go before you and
       I shall be a sign
   to guide my travelling,
       wandering race.
   You're the people of God."

3. "No matter what you may do,"
   the Lord said,
   "I shall be faithful and true,"
   the Lord said.
   "My love will strengthen you
       as you go along,
   for you're my travelling,
       wandering race.
   You're the people of God."

4. "Look at the birds in the air,"
   the Lord said,
   "They fly unhampered by care,"
   the Lord said.
   "You will move easier
       if you're travelling light,
   for you're a wandering,
       vagabond race.
   You're the people of God."

5. "Foxes have places to go,"
   the Lord said.
   "But I've no home here below,"
   the Lord said.
   "So if you want to be
       with me all your days,
   keep up the moving and
       travelling on.
   You're the people of God."

   Estelle White

198

1. Most ancient of all mysteries,
   before thy throne we lie;
   have mercy now, most merciful,
   most Holy Trinity.

2. When heaven and earth were yet
                           unmade,
   when time was yet unknown,
   thou, in thy bliss and majesty,
   didst live and love alone.

3. Thou wert not born; there was no
                           fount,
   from which thy being flowed;
   there is no end which thou canst
                           reach:
   but thou art simply God.

4. How wonderful creation is,
   the work that thou didst bless;
   and oh, what then must thou be like,
   Eternal Loveliness!

5. Most ancient of all mysteries,
   still at thy throne we lie;
   have mercy now, most merciful,
   most Holy Trinity.

   Frederick William Faber (1814-63)

2. Though poverty and work and woe
   the masters of my life may be,
   when times are worst, who does not
                           know
   darkness is light with love of thee?
   darkness is light with love of thee?

3. But scornful men have coldly said
   thy love was leading me from God;
   and yet in this I did but tread
   the very path my Saviour trod,
   the very path my Saviour trod.

4. They know but little of thy worth
   who speak these heartless words to
                           me;
   for what did Jesus love on earth
   one half so tenderly as thee?
   one half so tenderly as thee?

5. Get me the grace to love thee more;
   Jesus will give if thou wilt plead;
   and, Mother! when life's cares are
                           o'er,
   oh, I shall love thee then indeed!
   oh, I shall love thee then indeed!

6. Jesus, when his three hours were run,
   bequeath'd thee from the cross to me,
   and oh! how I love thy Son,
   sweet Mother! if I love not thee?
   sweet Mother! if I love not thee?

   Frederick William Faber (1814-63)

199

1. Mother of Mercy, day by day
   my love of thee grows more and
                           more;
   thy gifts are strewn upon my way,
   like sands upon the great seashore,
   like sands upon the great seashore.

200

1. *My glory and the lifter of my head,*
   my glory and the lifter of my head,
   for thou, O Lord, art a shield to me,
   my glory and the lifter of my head.
   I cried unto the Lord with my voice,
   I cried unto the Lord with my voice,
   I cried unto the Lord with my voice,
   and he heard me out of his holy hill.

   From Scripture

201

1. My God accept my heart this day,
   and make it wholly thine,
   that I from thee no more may stray,
   no more from thee decline.

2. Before the cross of him who died,
   behold, I prostrate fall;
   let every sin be crucified,
   and Christ be all in all.

3. Anoint me with thy heavenly grace,
   and seal me for thine own,
   that I may see thy glorious face,
   and worship at thy throne.

4. Let every thought, and work and
   word
   to thee be ever given,
   then life shall be thy service, Lord,
   and Death the gate of heaven.

5. All glory to the Father be,
   all glory to the Son,
   all glory, Holy Ghost, to thee,
   while endless ages run.

Matthew Bridges (1800-94)

202

1. My God, and is thy table spread,
   and does thy cup with love o'erflow?
   Thither be all thy children led,
   and let them all thy sweetness know.

2. Hail, sacred feast, which Jesus
   makes!
   Rich banquet of his flesh and blood!
   Thrice happy he, who here partakes
   that sacred stream, that heavenly
   food.

3. O let thy table honoured be,
   and furnished well with joyful
   guests;
   and may each soul salvation see,
   that here its sacred pledges tastes.

Philip Doddridge (1702-51)

203

1. My God, how wonderful thou art,
   thy majesty how bright
   how beautiful thy mercy-seat
   in depths of burning light.

2. How dread are thine eternal years
   O everlasting Lord!
   By prostrate spirits day and night
   incessantly adored.

3. How beautiful, how beautiful
   the sight of thee must be,
   thine endless wisdom, boundless
   power
   and awful purity!

4. Oh, how I fear thee, living God!
   with deepest, tenderest fears,
   and worship thee with trembling hope
   and penitential tears.

5. Yet I may love thee too, O Lord,
   almighty as thou art,
   for thou hast stooped to ask of me
   the love of my poor heart.

6. No earthly father loves like thee,
   no mother e'er so mild
   bears and forbears as thou hast done
   with me thy sinful child.

7. Father of Jesus, love's reward,
   what rapture will it be,
   prostrate before thy throne to lie,
   and gaze and gaze on thee!

Frederick William Faber (1814-63)

204

1. My God I love thee, not because
   I hope for heav'n thereby;
   nor yet that those who love thee not
   are lost eternally.

2. Thou, O my Jesus, thou didst me
   upon the cross embrace;
   for me didst bear the nails and spear
   and manifold disgrace.

3. And griefs and torments numberless
and sweat of agony;
e'en death itself — and all for one
who was thine enemy.

4. Then why, O Blessed Jesu Christ
should I not love thee well;
not for the sake of winning heaven,
or of escaping hell;

5. Not with the hope of gaining aught;
not seeking a reward,
but, as thyself hast loved me
O ever-loving Lord?

6. E'en so I love thee, and will love,
and in thy praise will sing;
solely because thou art my God
and my eternal king.

17th c., tr. Edward Caswall

205

1. My God loves me.
His love will never end.
He rests within my heart
for my God loves me.

2. His gentle hand
he stretches over me.
Though storm-clouds
threaten the day
he will set me free.

3. He comes to me
in sharing bread and wine.
He brings me life that will reach
past the end of time.

4. My God loves me,
his faithful love endures.
And I will live like a child
held in love secure.

5. The joys of love
as offerings now we bring.
The pains of love will be lost
in the praise we sing.

Verse 1 Anonymous
Verses 2-5 Sandra Joan Billington

206

1. My song is love unknown,
my Saviour's love to me,
love to the loveless shown,
that they might lovely be.
O who am I,
that for my sake,
my Lord should take
frail flesh and die?

2. He came from his blest throne,
salvation to bestow;
but men made strange, and none
the longed-for Christ would know,
but O, my friend,
my friend indeed,
who at my need
his life did spend!

3. Sometimes they strew his way,
and his sweet praises sing;
resounding all the day
hosannas to their King;
then 'Crucify!'
is all their breath,
and for his death
they thirst and cry.

4. Why, what hath my Lord done?
What makes this rage and spite?
He made the lame to run,
he gave the blind their sight.
Sweet injuries!
Yet they at these
themselves displease,
and 'gainst him rise.

5. They rise, and needs will have
my dear Lord made away;
a murderer they save,
the Prince of Life they slay.
Yet cheerful he
to suffering goes,
that he his foes
from thence might free.

6. In life, no house, no home
    my Lord on earth might have:
in death no friendly tomb
    but what a stranger gave.
What may I say?
Heaven was his home;
but mine the tomb
wherein he lay.

7. Here might I stay and sing,
    no story so divine,
never was love, dear King,
never was grief like thine.
This is my Friend,
in whose sweet praise
I all my days
could gladly spend.

Samuel Crossman (c. 1624-84)

207

1. New praises be given
    to Christ newly crowned,
who back to his heaven
    a new way hath found;
God's blessedness sharing
    before us he goes,
what mansions preparing,
    what endless repose!

2. His glory still praising
    on thrice holy ground
the apostles stood gazing,
    his mother around;
with hearts that beat faster,
    with eyes full of love,
they watched while their master
ascended above.

3. "No star can disclose him",
    the bright angels said;
"Eternity knows him,
    your conquering head;
those high habitations,
    he leaves not again,
till, judging all nations,
    on earth he shall reign".

4. Thus spoke they and straightway,
    where legions defend
heaven's glittering gateway,
    their Lord they attend,
and cry, looking thither,
    "Your portals let down
for him who rides hither
in peace and renown".

5. They asked, who keep sentry
    in that blessed town,
"Who thus claimeth entry,
    a king of renown?"
"The Lord of all valiance",
    that herald replied,
"Who Satan's battalions
    laid low in their pride".

6. Grant, Lord, that our longing
    may follow thee there,
on earth who are thronging
    thy temples with prayer;
and unto thee gather,
    Redeemer, thine own
where thou with thy Father
dost sit on the throne.

St. Bede the Venerable (673-735)
tr. R. A. Knox

208

1. Now come to me all you who seek
    and place your trust in me.
For I have comfort for the weak,
    the strength to set you free.
And, just as gentle blades of grass
can crack the hardened earth,
creation will be yours at last
when love is brought to birth.

2. Now come to me all you who seek
    and place your trust in me.
For I will comfort those who mourn
    and make the blind to see.
However dark the stormy night
the sun will raise the dawn,
and you will live beneath the light
of love in darkness born.

3. Now come to me all you who seek
and place your trust in me.
For I bring peace to those at war
and set the captives free.
Just as in cutting sun-ripe wheat
we count the summer's worth,
so shall all those who justice seek
be there at love's new birth.

Michael Cockett

209

1. Now Jesus said:
"We'll bake some bread,
so bring me flour and water.
Then bring me salt
and bring me yeast;
I'll bake for you a splendid feast,
and we will join and drink a toast
to friendship ever after."

2. They found the flour,
they found the salt,
they found a jug of water.
But, though they searched
around the town,
an ounce of yeast
could not be found.
They came to him
with eyes cast down
and told him of their failure.

3. Then Jesus said:
"Do not be sad,
we'll mix the flour and water.
And though we bake
unleavened bread,
if you will be the yeast instead,
the bread will rise up from the dead
and feed you ever after."

Michael Cockett

210

1. Now Jesus said:
"You must love one another,
pass it on, pass it on,"
And Jesus said:
"Call all men your brother,
come to me, learn to love,
pass it on, pass it on."

2. So Peter said:
"You must love one another,
pass it on, pass it on,"
So Peter said:
"Call all men your brother,
come to me, learn to love,
pass it on, pass it on."

3. The people said . . .

4. My Father said . . .

5. Now I can say . . .

Michael Cockett

211

1. Now thank we all our God,
with heart and hands and voices,
who wondrous things hath done,
in whom this world rejoices;
who from our mother's arms
hath blessed us on our way
with countless gifts of love,
and still is ours today.

2. O may this bounteous God
through all our life be near us
with ever joyful hearts
and blessed peace to cheer us;
and keep us in his grace,
and guide us when perplexed,
and free us from all ills
in this world and the next.

3. All praise and thanks to God
the Father now be given
the Son and him who reigns
with them in highest heaven,
the one Eternal God,
whom earth and heaven adore;
for thus it was, is now,
and shall be evermore.

Martin Rinkart (1586-1649),
tr. Catherine Winkworth

212

1. Now with the fast-departing light,
   maker of all! We ask of thee,
   of thy great mercy, through the
   night
   our guardian and defence to be.

2. Far off let idle visions fly;
   no phantom of the night molest:
   curb thou our raging enemy,
   that we in chaste repose may rest.

3. Father of mercies! hear our cry:
   hear us, O sole-begotten Son!
   Who, with the Holy Ghost most
   high,
   reignest while endless ages run.

   7th c., tr. Edward Caswall

213

1. O bread of heaven, beneath this veil
   thou dost my very God conceal;
   my Jesus, dearest treasure, hail;
   I love thee and adoring kneel;
   each loving soul by thee is fed
   with thine own self in form of bread.

2. O food of life, thou who dost give
   the pledge of immortality;
   I live; no, 'tis not I that live;
   God gives me life, God lives in me:
   he feeds my soul, he guides my ways,
   and every grief with joy repays.

3. O bond of love, that dost unite
   the servant to his living Lord;
   could I dare live, and not requite
   such love — then death were meet
   reward:
   I cannot live unless to prove
   some love for such unmeasured love.

4. Beloved Lord in heaven above,
   there, Jesus, thou awaitest me;
   to gaze on thee with changeless love,
   yes, thus I hope, thus shall it be:
   for how can he deny me heaven
   who here on earth himself hath
   given?

   St. Alphonsus (1696-1787)
   tr. Edward Vaughan

214

1. O come, all ye faithful,
   joyful and triumphant,
   O come ye, O come ye to Bethlehem;
   come and behold him,
   born the king of angels:

   O come, let us adore him,
   O come, let us adore him,
   O come, let us adore him,
   Christ the Lord.

2. God of God,
   light of light,
   lo! he abhors not the virgin's womb;
   very God,
   begotten not created:

3. Sing, choirs of angels,
   sing in exultation,
   sing all ye citizens of heaven above:
   glory to God
   in the highest:

4. Yea, Lord, we greet thee,
   born this happy morning,
   Jesu, to thee be glory given;
   word of the Father,
   now in flesh appearing:

   18th c., tr. Frederick Oakeley

215

1. O come and mourn with me awhile;
see, Mary calls us to her side;
O come and let us mourn with her;

Jesus our love, Jesus our love,
is crucified.

2. Have we no tears to shed for him,
while soldiers scoff and men deride?
Ah! look how patiently he hangs;

3. How fast his feet and hands are
nailed,
his blessed tongue with thirst is tied;
his failing eyes are blind with blood;

4. Seven times he spoke, seven words
of love,
and all three hours his silence cried.
For mercy on the souls of men;

5. O break, O break, hard heart of
mine:
thy weak self-love and guilty pride
his Pilate and his Judas were:

6. A broken heart, a fount of tears,
ask, and they will not be denied;
a broken heart, love's cradle is;

7. O love of God! O sin of man!
In this dread act your strength is
tried;
and victory remains with love;

Frederick William Faber (1814-63)

216

1. O come, O come, Emmanuel,
and ransom captive Israel,
that mourns in lonely exile here
until the Son of God appear:

Rejoice, rejoice! Emmanuel
shall come to thee, O Israel.

2. O come, thou Rod of Jesse, free
thine own from Satan's tyranny;
from depths of hell thy people save,
and give them vict'ry o'er the grave:

3. O come, thou dayspring, come and
cheer
our spirits by thine advent here;
disperse the gloomy clouds of night,
and death's dark shadows put to
flight:

4. O come, thou key of David, come
and open wide our heavenly home;
make safe the way that leads on high,
and close the path to misery.

5. O come, O come, thou Lord of
might,
who to thy tribes on Sinai's height
in ancient times didst give the law
in cloud and majesty and awe:

From the 'Great O Antiphons'
(12th-13th c.), tr. John Mason Neale

217

1. O Father, now the hour has come,
so glorify your Son,
that he may give eternal life
to those who hope in him.

2. Through Jesus Christ, your only Son,
the Word has now been sown,
so honour him with glory now,
the saviour of the world.

3. O Father of the Word of Truth,
the world has known you not,
but through the Son that you have
sent
your love is in our hearts.

4. He is no longer in this world,
he has returned to you.
So, holy Father, make us one
as he is one with you.

5. May all good men be joined as one,
as Father with the Son,
that through the unity of love,
the whole world may believe.

6. Through glory given to the Son,
the Father will reveal
the joy complete, the bond of love,
mysterious Three in One.

Michael Cockett

218

1. O Father, take in sign of love
   these gifts of bread and wine!
   With them we give our very selves,
   to be for ever thine!

2. These gifts another gift will be,
   thy Son in very deed,
   for us a willing victim made,
   the Lamb on whom we feed!

3. These are the gifts thy Son did bless
   the night before he died.
   By which he showed himself a priest
   and victim crucified!

4. He now has given us as our own
   his offering made to thee:
   his body broken, Blood outpoured,
   for us on Calvary!

5. This bread his Body will become,
   this wine his Blood will be!
   Our humble gifts will be the gift
   that is most dear to thee!

6. This perfect gift thou wilt restore
   to greatest and to least,
   to make all one in love and joy
   in thy communion-feast!

James Quinn, S.J.

219

1. Of the glorious body telling,
   O my tongue, its myst'ries sing,
   and the blood, all price excelling,
   which the world's eternal king,
   in a noble womb once dwelling,
   shed for this world's ransoming.

2. Giv'n for us, for us descending,
   of a virgin to proceed,
   man with man in converse blending,
   scattered he the gospel seed,
   'till his sojourn drew to ending,
   which he closed in wondrous deed.

3. At the last great supper lying,
   circled by his brethren's band,
   meekly with the law complying,
   first, he finished its command.

Then, immortal food supplying,
gave himself with his own hand.

4. Word made flesh, by word he
                              maketh
   very bread his flesh to be;
   man in wine Christ's blood
                              partaketh,
   and if senses fail to see,
   faith alone the true heart waketh,
   to behold the mystery.

5. Therefore, we before him bending,
   this great sacrament revere;
   types and shadows have their ending,
   for the newer rite is here;
   faith, our outward sense befriending,
   makes the inward vision clear.

6. Glory let us give, and blessing,
   to the Father and the Son;
   honour, might and praise addressing,
   while eternal ages run;
   ever too his love confessing,
   who from both, with both is one.

St. Thomas Aquinas (1127-74),
tr. J. M. Neale, E. Caswall and others

220

1. O Godhead hid, devoutly I adore
      thee,
   who truly art within the forms
      before me;
   to thee my heart I bow with
      bended knee,
   as failing quite in contemplating
      thee.

2. Sight, touch, and taste in thee are
      each deceived,
   the ear alone most safely is
      believed:
   I believe all the Son of God has
      spoken;
   than truth's own word there is no
      truer token.

3. God only on the cross lay hid from
      view;
   but here lies hid at once the
      manhood too:

and I, in both professing my belief,
make the same prayer as the
repentant thief.

4. Thy wounds, as Thomas saw, I do
   not see;
   yet thee confess my Lord and God
   to be;
   make me believe thee ever more and
   more,
   In thee my hope, in thee my love to
   store.

5. O thou memorial of our Lord's own
   dying!
   O bread that living art and vivifying!
   Make ever thou my soul on thee to
   live;
   ever a taste of heavenly sweetness
   give.

6. O loving Pelican! O Jesus, Lord!
   Unclean I am, but cleanse me in thy
   blood;
   of which a single drop, for sinners
   spilt,
   is ransom for a world's entire guilt.

7. Jesus, whom for the present veiled
   I see,
   what I so thirst for, oh, vouchsafe
   to me:
   that I may see thy countenance
   unfolding,
   and may be blest thy glory in
   beholding.

St. Thomas Aquinas (1227-74),
tr. Edward Caswall

221

1. O God of earth and altar,
   bow down and hear our cry,
   our earthly rulers falter,
   our people drift and die;
   the walls of gold entomb us,
   the swords of scorn divide,
   take not thy thunder from us,
   but take away our pride.

2. From all that terror teaches,
   from lies of tongue and pen,
   from all the easy speeches

that comfort cruel men,
from sale and profanation
of honour and the sword,
from sleep and from damnation,
deliver us, good Lord!

3. Tie in a living tether
   the prince and priest and thrall,
   bind all our lives together,
   smite us and save us all;
   in ire and exultation
   aflame with faith, and free,
   lift up a living nation,
   a single sword to thee.

G. K. Chesterton (1874-1936)

222

1. O God, our help in ages past,
   our hope for years to come,
   our shelter from the stormy blast,
   and our eternal home;

2. Beneath the shadow of thy throne,
   thy saints have dwelt secure;
   sufficient is thine arm alone,
   and our defence is sure.

3. Before the hills in order stood,
   or earth received her frame,
   from everlasting thou art God,
   to endless years the same.

4. A thousand ages in thy sight,
   are like an evening gone;
   short as the watch that ends the
                                night
   before the rising sun.

5. Time, like an ever-rolling stream,
   bears all its sons away;
   they fly forgotten, as a dream
   dies at the opening day.

6. O God, our help in ages past,
   our hope for years to come,
   be thou our guard while troubles
                                last,
   and our eternal home.

Isaac Watts (1674-1748)

223

1. O God, thy people gather,
   obedient to thy word,
   around thy holy altar,
   to praise thy name, O Lord;
   for all thy loving kindness
   our grateful hearts we raise;
   but pardon first the blindness
   of all our sinful ways.

2. Thou art our loving Father,
   thou art our holiest Lord,
   but we have sinned against thee,
   by thought and deed and word.
   Before the court of heaven
   we stand and humbly pray
   our sins may be forgiven,
   our faults be washed away.

3. Though sinful, we implore thee
   to turn and make us live,
   that so we may adore thee,
   and our due offering give,
   and may the prayers and voices
   of thy glad people rise,
   as thy whole Church rejoices
   in this great sacrifice.

   Anthony Nye

224

1. O God, we give ourselves today
   with this pure host to thee,
   the selfsame gift which thy dear Son
   gave once on Calvary.

2. Entire and whole, our life and love
   with heart and soul and mind,
   for all our sins and faults and needs,
   thy Church and all mankind.

3. With humble and with contrite heart
   this bread and wine we give
   because thy Son once gave himself
   and died that we might live.

4. Though lowly now, soon by thy
   word
   these offered gifts will be
   the very body of our Lord,
   his soul and deity.

5. His very body, offered up
   a gift beyond all price,
   he gives to us, that we may give
   in loving sacrifice.

6. O Lord, who took our human life,
   as water mixed with wine,
   grant through this sacrifice that we
   may share thy life divine.

   Anthony Nye

225

Oh living water, refresh my soul.
Oh living water, refresh my soul
Spirit of joy, Lord of creation.
Spirit of hope, Spirit of peace.

1. Spirit of God,
   Spirit of God.

2. Oh set us free,
   Oh set us free.

3. Come, pray in us,
   come, pray in us.

   Rosalie Vissing

226

1. Oh Lord,
   all the world belongs to you,
   and you are always making
   all things new.
   What is wrong you forgive,
   and the new life you give
   is what's turning the world
   upside down.

2. The world's
   only loving to its friends,
   but you have brought us love that
   never ends;
   loving enemies too,
   and this loving with you
   is what's turning the world
   upside down.

3. This world
   lives divided and apart.
   You draw all men together
   and we start
   in your body to see
   that in fellowship we

can be turning the world
upside down.

4. The world
wants the wealth to live in state,
but you show us a new way
to be great:
like a servant you came,
and if we do the same,
we'll be turning the world
upside down.

5. Oh Lord
all the world belongs to you,
and you are always making
all things new.
Send your Spirit on all
in your Church whom you call
to be turning the world
upside down.

Patrick Appleford

227

1. O Lord, my God,
when I in awesome wonder,
consider all the worlds
thy hand has made,
I see the stars,
I hear the rolling thunder,
thy pow'r throughout
the universe displayed.

Then sings my soul,
my Saviour God to thee:
How great thou art,
how great thou art.
Then sings my soul,
my Saviour God to thee:
How great thou art,
how great thou art.

2. And when I think
that God, his Son not sparing,
sent him to die, I
scarce can take it in
that on the cross,
my burden gladly bearing,
he bled and died
to take away my sin.

3. When Christ shall come
with shout of acclamation
and take me home,
what joy shall fill my heart;
when I shall bow
in humble adoration,
and there proclaim;
my God, how great thou art.

Unknown

228

1. O holy Lord, by all adored,
our trespasses confessing,
to thee this day thy children pray,
our holy faith professing!
Accept, O king, the gifts we bring,
our songs of praise, the prayers we
raise,
and grant us, Lord, thy blessing.

2. To God on high be thanks and
praise,
who deigns our bond to sever;
his care shall guide us all our days,
and harm shall reach us never,
on him we rest with faith assured;
of all that live he is the Lord,
for ever and for ever.

M. F. Bell (1862-1947)

229

1. Oh sinner man,
where you going to run to?
Oh, sinner man,
where you going to run to?
Oh, sinner man,
where you going to run to?
all on that day?

2. Run to the moon,
moon won't you hide me?
Run to the sea,
sea won't you hide me?
Run to the sun,
sun won't you hide me?
all on that day?

3. Lord said: "Sinner Man,
    the moon'll be a-bleeding."
   Lord said: "Sinner Man,
    the sea'll be a-sinking."
   Lord said: "Sinner Man,
    the sun'll be a-freezing."
   all on that day.

4. Run to the Lord:
    "Lord, won't you hide me?"
   Run to the Lord:
    "Lord, won't you hide me?"
   Run to the Lord:
    "Lord, won't you hide me?"
   all on that day.

5. Lord said: "Sinner Man,
    you should have been a-praying!"
   Lord said: "Sinner Man,
    you should have been a-praying!"
   Lord said: "Sinner Man,
    you should have been a-praying!"
   all on that day.

Traditional

230

1. Oh, the Lord looked down
    from his window in the sky,
   said: "I created man
    but I can't remember why!
   Nothing but fighting
    since creation day.
   I'll send a little water
    and wash them all away."
   Oh, the Lord came down
    and looked around a spell.
   There was Mister Noah
    behaving mighty well.
   And that is the reason
    the Scriptures record
   Noah found grace
    in the eyes of the Lord.

   Noah found grace
    in the eyes of the Lord.
   Noah found grace
    in the eyes of the Lord.
   Noah found grace
    in the eyes of the Lord
   and he left him high and dry.

2. The Lord said: "Noah,
    there's going to be a flood,
   there's going to be some water,
    there's going to be some mud,
   so take off your hat, Noah,
    take off your coat,
   get Sham, Ham and Japhat
    and build yourself a boat."
   Noah said: "Lord,
    I don't believe I could."
   The Lord said: "Noah,
    get yourself some wood.
   You never know what
    you can do till you try.
   Build it fifty cubits wide
    and thirty cubits high."

3. Noah said: "There she is,
    there she is Lord!"
   The Lord said: "Noah,
    it's time to get aboard.
   Take of each creature
    a he and a she
   and of course take Mrs Noah
    and the whole family."
   Noah said: "Lord,
    it's getting mighty dark."
   The Lord said: "Noah,
    get those creatures in the ark."
   Noah said: "Lord,
    it's beginning to pour."
   The Lord said: "Noah,
    hurry up and close the door."

4. The ark rose up
    on the bosom of the deep.
   After forty days
    Mr Noah took a peep.
   He said: "We're not moving, Lord,
    where are we at?"
   The Lord said: "You're sitting
    right on Mount Ararat."
   Noah said: "Lord,
    it's getting nice and dry."
   The Lord said: "Noah,
    see my rainbow in the sky.
   Take all your creatures
    and people the earth
   and be sure that you're not
    more trouble than you're worth."

231

1. Oh, the love of my Lord
   is the essence
   of all that I love here on earth.
   All the beauty I see
   he has given to me
   and his giving is gentle as silence.

2. Every day, every hour,
   every moment
   have been blessed by
   the strength of his love.
   At the turn of each tide
   he is there at my side,
   and his touch is as gentle as silence.

3. There've been times when I've turned
   from his presence,
   and I've walked other paths,
   other ways.
   But I've called on his name
   in the dark of my shame,
   and his mercy was gentle as silence.

   Estelle White

232

1. Oh when the saints go marching in,
   oh when the saints go marching in,
   I want to be in that number,
   when the saints go marching in.

2. Oh when the drums begin to bang,
   oh when the drums begin to bang,
   I want to be in that number,
   when the drums begin to bang.

3. Oh when the stars fall from the sky,
   oh when the stars fall from the sky,
   I want to be in that number,
   when the stars fall from the sky.

4. Oh when the moon turns into blood,
   oh when the moon turns into blood,
   I want to be in that number,
   when the moon turns into blood.

5. Oh when the sun turns into fire,
   oh when the sun turns into fire,
   I want to be in that number,
   when the sun turns into fire.

6. Oh when the fires begin to blaze,
   oh when the fires begin to blaze,
   I want to be in that number,
   when the fires begin to blaze.

7. Oh when the Lord calls out the
   names,
   oh when the Lord calls out the
   names,
   I want to be in that number,
   when the Lord calls out the names.

   Traditional

233

1. O Jesus Christ, remember,
   when thou shalt come again,
   upon the clouds of heaven,
   with all thy shining train;
   when every eye shall see thee
   in deity revealed,
   who now upon this altar
   in silence art concealed.

2. Remember then, O Saviour,
   I supplicate of thee,
   that here I bowed before thee
   upon my bended knee;
   that here I owned thy presence,
   and did not thee deny,
   and glorified thy greatness
   though hid from human eye.

3. Accept, divine Redeemer,
   the homage of my praise;
   be thou the light and honour
   and glory of my days.
   Be thou my consolation
   when death is drawing nigh;
   be thou my only treasure
   through all eternity.

   Edward Caswall (1814-78)

234

1. O king of might and splendour
   creator most adored,
   this sacrifice we render
   to thee as sov'reign Lord.
   May these our gifts be pleasing
   unto thy majesty,

mankind from sin releasing
who have offended thee.

2. Thy body thou hast given,
thy blood thou hast outpoured,
that sin might be forgiven,
O Jesus, loving Lord.
As now with love most tender,
thy death we celebrate,
our lives in self-surrender
to thee we consecrate.

Dom Gregory Murray, O.S.B.

235

1. O little town of Bethlehem,
how still we see thee lie!
Above thy deep and dreamless sleep
the silent stars go by.
Yet, in thy dark streets shineth
the everlasting light;
the hopes and fears of all the years
are met in thee tonight.

2. O morning stars, together
proclaim the holy birth,
and praises sing to God the King,
and peace to men on earth;
for Christ is born of Mary;
and, gathered all above,
while mortals sleep, the angels keep
their watch of wondering love.

3. How silently, how silently,
the wondrous gift is given!
So God imparts to human hearts
the blessings of his heaven.
No ear may hear his coming;
but in this world of sin,
where meek souls will receive him, still
the dear Christ enters in.

4. Where children pure and happy
pray to the blessed Child,
where misery cries out to thee,
Son of the mother mild;
where charity stands watching
and faith holds wide the door,
the dark night wakes, the glory
breaks,
and Christmas comes once more.

Phillips Brooks (1835-93)

236

1. O Mother blest, whom God bestows
on sinners and on just,
what joy, what hope thou givest
those
who in thy mercy trust.

Thou art clement, thou art chaste,
Mary, thou art fair;
of all mothers sweetest, best;
none with thee compare.

2. O heavenly mother, mistress sweet!
It never yet was told
that suppliant sinner left thy feet
unpitied, unconsoled.

3. O mother pitiful and mild,
cease not to pray for me;
for I do love thee as a child,
and sigh for love of thee.

4. Most powerful mother, all men
know
thy Son denies thee nought;
thou askest, wishest it, and lo!
his power thy will hath wrought.

5. O mother blest, for me obtain
ungrateful though I be,
to love that God who first could
deign
to show such love for me.

St. Alphonsus Liquori (1699-1787),
tr. Edmund Vaughan

237

1. O my Lord, within my heart
pride will have no home,
every talent that I have
comes from you alone.

And like a child at rest
close to its mother's breast,
safe in your arms
my soul is calmed.

2. Lord, my eyes do not look high
nor my thoughts take wings,
for I can find treasures in
ordinary things.

3. Great affairs are not for me,
   deeds beyond my scope,
   in the simple things I do
   I find joy and hope.

   Estelle White

238

1. Once in royal David's city
   stood a lowly cattle shed,
   where a Mother laid her baby
   in a manger for his bed:
   Mary was that Mother mild,
   Jesus Christ her little child.

2. He came down to earth from
   heaven,
   who is God and Lord of all,
   and his shelter was a stable
   and his cradle was a stall;
   with the poor, and mean, and lowly,
   lived on earth our Saviour holy.

3. And through all his wondrous
   childhood
   he would honour and obey,
   love, and watch the lowly maiden
   in whose gentle arms he lay;
   Christian children all must be
   mild, obedient, good as he.

4. For he is our childhood's pattern,
   day by day like us he grew;
   he was little, weak and helpless,
   tears and smiles like us he knew;
   and he feeleth for our sadness,
   and he shareth in our gladness.

5. And our eyes at last shall see him
   through his own redeeming love,
   for that child so dear and gentle
   is our Lord in heaven above;
   and he leads his children on
   to the place where he is gone.

6. Not in that poor lowly stable,
   with the oxen standing by,
   we shall see him; but in heaven,
   set at God's right hand on high;
   when like stars his children crowned
   all in white shall wait around.

   Cecil Francis Alexander (1818-95)

239

1. On Jordan's bank the Baptist's cry
   announces that the Lord is nigh,
   come then and hearken, for he
   brings
   glad tidings from the King of kings.

2. Then cleansed be every Christian
   breast,
   and furnished for so great a guest!
   Yea, let us each our hearts prepare,
   for Christ to come and enter there.

3. For thou art our salvation, Lord,
   our refuge and our great reward;
   without thy grace our souls must
   fade,
   and wither like a flower decayed.

4. Stretch forth thy hand, to heal our
   sore,
   and make us rise, to fall no more;
   once more upon thy people shine,
   and fill the world with love divine.

5. All praise, eternal Son, to thee
   whose advent sets thy people free,
   whom, with the Father, we adore,
   and Holy Ghost, for evermore.

   C. Coffin (1676-1749), tr. J. Chandler

240

1. On this house your blessing, Lord.
On this house your grace bestow.
On this house your blessing, Lord.
May it come and never go.
Bringing peace and joy
and happiness,
bringing love that knows no end.
On this house your blessing Lord.
On this house your blessing send.

2. On this house your loving, Lord.
May it overflow each day.
' On this house your loving, Lord.
May it come and with us stay.
Drawing us in love
and unity
by the love received from you.
On this house your loving, Lord.
May it come each day anew.

3. On this house your giving, Lord.
May it turn and ever flow.
On this house your giving, Lord.
On this house your wealth bestow.
Filling all our hopes
and wishes, Lord.
in the way you know is best.
On this house your giving, Lord.
May it come and with us rest.

4. On this house your calling, Lord.
May it come to us each day.
On this house your calling, Lord.
May it come to lead the way.
Filling us with nobler
yearnings, Lord,
calling us to live in you.
On this house your calling, Lord.
May it come each day anew.

Sister M. Pereira

241

1. Onward, Christian soldiers,
marching as to war,
with the Cross of Jesus
going on before.
Christ the royal Master
leads against the foe;
forward into battle,
see, his banners go!

Onward, Christian soldiers,
marching as to war,
with the Cross of Jesus
going on before.

2. At the sign of triumph
Satan's legions flee;
on then, Christian soldiers,
on to victory.
Hell's foundations quiver
at the shout of praise;
brothers, lift your voices,
loud your anthem raise.

3. Like a mighty army
moves the Church of God.
Brothers, we are treading
where the Saints have trod;
we are not divided,
all one body we,
one in hope and doctrine,
one in charity.

4. Crowns and thrones may perish,
kingdoms rise and wane,
but the Church of Jesus
constant will remain;
gates of hell can never
'gainst that Church prevail;
we have Christ's own promise,
and that cannot fail.

5. Onward, then, ye people,
join our happy throng,
blend with ours your voices
in the triumph song;
glory, laud, and honour
unto Christ the King;
this through countless ages
men and angels sing.

S. Baring-Gould (1834-1924)

242

1. Open your ears, O Christian people,
   open your ears and hear Good News.
   Open your hearts
      O royal priesthood
   God has come to you.
   God has spoken to his people,
   alleluia.
   And his words are words of wisdom,
   alleluia.

2. Israel comes to greet the Saviour,
   Judah is glad to see his day.
   From East and West
      the peoples travel,
   he will show the way.

3. He who has ears to hear his message;
   he who has ears, then let him hear.
   He who would learn
      the way of wisdom,
   let him hear God's words.

                                    W. F. Jabusch

243

1. O perfect love,
      all human thought transcending,
   lowly we kneel
      in prayer before thy throne.
   That theirs may be
      the love which knows no ending
   whom thou for evermore
      dost join in one.

2. O perfect life,
      be thou their full assurance
   of tender charity
      and steadfast faith,
   of patient hope,
      and quiet, brave endurance,
   with childlike trust
      that fears nor pain nor death.

3. Grant them the joy
      which brightens earthly sorrow,
   grant them the peace
      which calms all earthly strife;
   and to life's day
      the glorious unknown morrow
   that dawns upon
      eternal love and life.

Dorothy Francis Gurney (1858-1932)

244

1. O praise ye the Lord!
      praise him in the height;
   rejoice in his word,
      ye angels of light;
   ye heavens, adore him,
      by whom ye were made,
   and worship before him,
      in brightness arrayed.

2. O praise ye the Lord!
      praise him upon earth,
   in tuneful accord,
      ye sons of new birth.
   Praise him who hath brought you
      his grace from above,
   praise him who hath taught you
      to sing of his love.

3. O praise ye the Lord,
      all things that give sound;
   each jubilant chord
      re-echo around;
   loud organs, his glory
      forth tell in deep tone,
   and, sweet harp, the story
      of what he hath done.

4. O praise ye the Lord!
      thanksgiving and song
   to him be outpoured
      all ages along;
   for love in creation,
      for heaven restored,
   for grace of salvation,
      O praise ye the Lord!

Henry Williams Baker (1821-77),
based on Psalms 148 and 150

245

1. O Priest and Victim, Lord of life,
   throw wide the gates of paradise!
   We face our foes in mortal strife;
   thou art our strength:
   O heed our cries!

2. To Father, Son and Spirit blest,
   one only God, be ceaseless praise!
   May he in goodness grant us rest
   in heav'n, our home,
   for endless days!

   St Thomas Aquinas (1227-74)
   tr. James Quinn, S.J.

246

1. O purest of creatures!
   Sweet mother, sweet maid;
   the one spotless womb
   wherein Jesus was laid.
   Dark night hath come down
   on us, mother, and we
   look out for thy shining,
   sweet star of the sea.

2. Deep night hath come down on
   this rough-spoken world.
   And the banners of darkness
   are boldly unfurled;
   and the tempest-tossed Church,
   all her eyes are on thee.
   They look to thy shining,
   sweet star of the sea.

3. He gazed on thy soul,
   it was spotless and fair;
   for the empire of sin,
   it had never been there;
   none ever had owned thee,
   dear mother, but he,
   and he blessed thy clear shining,
   sweet star of the sea.

4. Earth gave him one lodging;
   'twas deep in thy breast,
   and God found a home where
   the sinner finds rest;
   his home and his hiding-place,
   both were in thee;
   he was won by thy shining,
   sweet star of the sea.

5. Oh, blissful and calm
   was the wonderful rest
   that thou gavest thy God
   in thy virginal breast;
   for the heaven he left
   he found heaven in thee,
   and he shone in thy shining,
   sweet star of the sea.

   Frederick William Faber (1814-63)

247

1. O sacred head sore wounded,
   defiled and put to scorn,
   O kingly head surrounded
   with mocking crown of thorn,
   what sorrow mars thy grandeur?
   Can death thy bloom deflower?
   O countenance whose splendour
   the hosts of heaven adore.

2. Thy beauty, long-desirèd,
   hath vanished from our sight;
   thy power is all expirèd,
   and quenched the light of light.
   Ah me! for whom thou diest,
   hide not so far thy grace:
   show me, O love most highest,
   the brightness of thy face.

3. I pray thee, Jesu, own me,
   me, shepherd good, for thine;
   who to thy fold hast won me,
   and fed with truth divine.
   Me guilty, me refuse not;
   incline thy face to me,
   this comfort that I lose not
   on earth to comfort thee.

4. In thy most bitter passion
   my heart to share doth cry,
   with thee for my salvation
   upon the cross to die.
   Ah, keep my heart thus movèd
   to stand thy cross beneath,
   to mourn thee, well-beloved,
   yet thank thee for thy death.

5. My days are few, O fail not,
with thine immortal power,
to hold me that I quail not
in death's most fearful hour:
that I may fight befriended,
and see in my last strife
to me thine arms extended
upon the cross of life.

*Paulus Gerhardt (1607-76),
tr. Robert Bridges*

248

1. O Sacred Heart,
our home lies deep in thee;
on earth thou art an exile's rest,
in heav'n the glory of the blest,
O Sacred Heart.

2. O Sacred Heart,
thou fount of contrite tears;
where'er those living waters flow,
new life to sinners they bestow,
O Sacred Heart.

3. O Sacred Heart,
bless our dear native land;
may England's sons in truth e'er
stand,
with faith's bright banner still in
hand,
O Sacred Heart.

4. O Sacred Heart,
our trust is all in thee,
for though earth's night be dark
and drear,
thou breathest rest where thou art
near,
O Sacred Heart.

5. O Sacred Heart,
when shades of death shall fall,
receive us 'neath thy gentle care,
and save us from the tempter's snare,
O Sacred Heart.

6. O Sacred Heart,
lead exiled children home,
where we may ever rest near thee,
in peace and joy eternally,
O Sacred Heart.

Francis Stanfield (1835-1914)

249

1. O thou, who at
thy Eucharist didst pray
that all thy Church
might be for ever one.
grant us at every
Eucharist to say
with longing heart and soul,
"Thy will be done".
O may we all one bread,
one body be,
one through this sacrament of unity.

2. For all thy Church,
O Lord, we intercede;
make thou our sad
divisions soon to cease;
draw us the nearer
each to each, we plead,
by drawing all to thee,
O Prince of peace;
thus may we all one
bread, one body be,
one through this sacrament of unity.

3. We pray thee too
for wanderers from thy fold,
O bring them back,
good shepherd of the sheep,
back to the faith which
saints believed of old,
back to the Church which still
that faith doth keep;
soon may we all one bread,
one body be,
one through this sacrament of unity.

4. So, Lord, at length
    When sacraments shall cease,
    may we be one
      with all thy Church above,
    one with thy saints in
      one unbroken peace,
    one with thy saints in one
      unbounded love:
    more blessed still, in peace
      and love to be
    one with the Trinity in unity.

William Harry Turton (1856-1938)

250

1. O Trinity, most blessed light,
    O unity of sovereign might,
    as now the fiery sun departs,
    shed thou thy beams within our
                                hearts.

2. To thee our morning song of praise,
    to thee our evening prayer we raise;
    thee may our souls for evermore,
    in lowly reverence adore.

3. All praise to God the Father be,
    all praise, eternal Son, to thee,
    whom with the Spirit we adore,
    for ever and for evermore.

St. Ambrose (340-397), tr. J. M. Neale

251

1. Our Father, who art in heaven,
    hallowed be thy name.
    Thy kingdom come thy will be
                                done,
    hallowed be thy name,
    hallowed be thy name.

2. On earth as it is in heaven,
    hallowed be thy name.
    Give us this day our daily bread,
    hallowed be thy name,
    hallowed be thy name.

3. Forgive us our trespasses,
    hallowed be thy name,
    as we forgive those who trespass
                                against us,
    hallowed be thy name,
    hallowed be thy name.

4. And lead us not into temptation,
    hallowed be thy name,
    but deliver us from all that is evil,
    hallowed be thy name,
    hallowed be thy name.

5. For thine is the kingdom, the power
                            and the glory,
    hallowed be thy name,
    for ever, and for ever and ever,
    hallowed be thy name,
    hallowed be thy name.

6. Amen, amen, it shall be so,
    hallowed be thy name.
    Amen, amen, it shall be so,
    hallowed be thy name,
    hallowed be thy name.

Traditional Caribbean

252

1. Out and away
      the mountains are calling!
    Voices are clear
      and wide as the sky!
    Where is the music
      I hear in my heart:
    soars over valleys
      as swift as a lark;
    echoes the joy that has
      scattered the dark: I am free.

2. Hear the wind sigh
      through leaves that are falling;
    see the wind sway
      the trees that are dry.
    Silent the darkness
      where thunder-clouds form;
    still is the world as
      it waits for the storm:
    now comes the lightning that
      heralds the dawn of the rain.

3. Water is clear,
as clear as the moonlight;
dew on the ground,
a tear in the eye.
Rivers and torrents
have vanished before;
oceans have coastlines
and continents shores:
Boundless the flow that's
unlocking the doors of my heart.

4. Free as the day
my spirit is flying:
eagles have wings,
but none strong as these!
Where have I found it,
this life newly-grown?
Gently, my heart says
it's not of my own:
deeper beyond me the Spirit
has blown — he is love.

John Glynn

253

1. O worship the King
all glorious above;
O gratefully sing
his power and his love:
our shield and defender,
the ancient of days,
pavilioned in splendour,
and girded with praise.

2. O tell of his might,
O sing of his grace,
whose robe is the light,
whose canopy space.
His chariots of wrath,
the deep thunder-clouds form,
and dark is his path
on the wings of the storm.

3. This earth, with its store
of wonders untold,
almighty, thy power
hath founded of old;
hath stablished it fast
by a changeless decree,
and round it hath cast,
like a mantle, the sea.

4. Thy bountiful care
what tongue can recite?
It breathes in the air,
it shines in the light;
it streams from the hills,
it descends to the plain,
and sweetly distils
in the dew and the rain.

5. Frail children of dust,
and feeble as frail,
in thee do we trust,
nor find thee to fail;
thy mercies how tender!
How firm to the end!
Our maker, defender,
redeemer, and friend.

6. O measureless might,
ineffable love,
while angels delight
to hymn thee above,
thy humbler creation,
though feeble their lays,
with true adoration
shall sing to thy praise.

Robert Grant (1779-1838)

254

1. Peace is flowing like a river,
flowing out through you and me,
spreading out into the desert,
setting all the captives free.

2. Love is flowing like a river . . .

3. Joy is flowing like a river . . .

4. Hope is flowing like a river . . .

Anonymous

255

1. Peace is the gift of heaven to earth,
   softly enfolding our fears.
   Peace is the gift of
      Christ to the world,
   given for us.
   He is the Lamb who bore
      the pain of peace.

2. Peace is the gift of Christ
      to his Church,
   wound of the lance of his love.
   Love is the pain he
      suffered for man,
   offered to us:
   Oh, to accept the wound
      that brings us peace!

3. Joy is the gift the Spirit imparts,
   born of the heavens and earth.
   We are his children,
      children of joy,
   people of God:
   He is our Lord, our peace,
      our love, our joy!

John Glynn

256

*Peacemakers to be called
   the sons of God.
Peacemakers to be called
   the sons of God.*

1. Seeing the crowd,
   Jesus went up to the hill.
   There he sat down
   and was joined by his friends.
   Then he began to speak to them
   and this is what he said:
   You must be . . .

2. Happy the gentle,
   for I give to them the earth.
   Happy the mourners,
   I will comfort their distress.
   Happy are those who thirst and
   hunger after what is right.
   They shall be . . .

Malcolm Campbell-Carr

257

1. Peace, perfect peace,
      is the gift of Christ our Lord.
   Peace, perfect peace,
      is the gift of Christ our Lord.
   Thus, says the Lord
      will the world know my friends.
   Peace, perfect peace,
      is the gift of Christ our Lord.

2. Love, perfect love . . .

3. Faith, perfect faith . . .

4. Hope, perfect hope ... .

5. Joy, perfect joy . . .

Kevin Mayhew

258

1. People of God,
      give praise to his name,
   praise everlasting is his,
   brought to his feast
      as guests in his house,
   praise everlasting is his,
   enter with joy, the Spirit is here,
   praise everlasting is his,
   gladly receive the word that is life,
   praise everlasting is his.

2. Sing with one voice,
      one love in your heart,
   praise everlasting is his,
   love that the Saviour
      bears to us all;
   praise everlasting is his,
   friend for the friendless, neighbour
      for foe,
   praise everlasting is his,
   Christ for all peoples, we are his sign,
   praise everlasting is his.

3. All that we have
   and all that we are,
   praise everlasting is his,
   all is his gift,
   his token of love,
   praise everlasting is his,
   all to be loved, made profit for love,
   praise everlasting is his,
   all to be taken home to the Lord,
   praise everlasting is his.

4. Praise for his glory,
   thanks for his gifts,
   praise everlasting is his,
   God everlasting, one that is three,
   praise everlasting is his,
   offer him praise,
   the Lord of all might,
   praise everlasting is his,
   majesty, glory, age upon age,
   praise everlasting is his.

Luke Connaughton

259

1. Praise him, praise him,
   praise him in the morning,
   praise him in the noontime.
   Praise him, praise him,
   praise him when the sun goes down.

2. Love him, . . .

3. Trust him, . . .

4. Serve him, . . .

5. Jesus, . . .

Anonymous

260

1. Praise, my soul, the king of heaven!
   To his feet thy tribute bring.
   Ransomed, healed, restored, forgiven,
   who like me his praise should sing?
   Praise him! Praise him!
   Praise him! Praise him!
   Praise the everlasting king!

2. Praise him for his grace and favour
   to our fathers in distress;

praise him still the same for ever,
slow to chide and swift to bless.
Praise him! Praise him!
Praise him! Praise him!
Glorious in his faithfulness!

3. Father-like he tends and spares us;
   well our feeble frame he knows;
   in his hands he gently bears us,
   rescues us from all our foes.
   Praise him! Praise him!
   Praise him! Praise him!
   Widely as his mercy flows!

4. Angels, help us to adore him;
   ye behold him face to face;
   sun and moon bow down before
                              him,
   dwellers all in time and space.
   Praise him! Praise him!
   Praise him! Praise him!
   Praise with us the God of grace!

Henry Francis Lyte (1793-1847)

261

Praise the Lord, and sing hallelujah,
hallelujah, hallelujah.
Praise the Lord, and sing hallelujah,
hallelujah, hallelujah.

1. Praise him for the sun and
   for the stars above,
   hallelujah, hallelujah.
   Praise him with your brothers
   for he is the God of love,
   hallelujah, hallelujah.

2. Praise him when you're happy,
   praise him when you're sad,
   hallelujah, hallelujah.
   He's the God who saves us
   and his message makes us glad,
   hallelujah, hallelujah.

3. Praise him in the morning,
   praise him in the night,
   hallelujah, hallelujah.
   Praise him in the thunder
   for he is the God of might,
   hallelujah, hallelujah.

Gerald O'Mahony

262

1. Praise to the Holiest in the height,
   and in the depth be praise,
   in all his words most wonderful,
   most sure in all his ways.

2. O loving wisdom of our God!
   When all was sin and shame,
   a second Adam to the fight,
   and to the rescue came.

3. O wisest love! that flesh and blood
   which did in Adam fail,
   should strive afresh against the foe,
   should strive and should prevail;

4. And that a higher gift than grace
   should flesh and blood refine,
   God's presence and his very self,
   and Essence all divine.

5. O generous love! that he who smote
   in man for man the foe,
   the double agony in man
   for man should undergo.

6. And in the garden secretly
   and on the Cross on high,
   should teach his brethren, and
   inspire
   to suffer and to die.

7. Praise to the Holiest in the height,
   and in the depth be praise,
   in all his words most wonderful,
   most sure in all his ways.

   John Henry Newman (1801-90)

263

Praise to the Lord our God,
let us sing together,
lifting our hearts and our voices
to sing with joy and gladness.
Come along, along, along,
and sing with . . .

Estelle White

264

1. Praise to the Lord, the Almighty,
   the King of creation!
   O my soul, praise him,
   for he is your health and
   salvation.
   All you who hear,
   now to his altar draw near,
   join in profound adoration.

2. Praise to the Lord, let us offer
   our gifts at his altar;
   let not our sins and transgressions
   now cause us to falter.
   Christ, the High Priest,
   bids us all join in his feast.
   Victims with him on the altar.

3. Praise to the Lord, oh, let all that
   is in us adore him!
   All that has life and breath,
   come now in praises before him.
   Let the Amen sound from
   his people again,
   now as we worship before him.

   Joachim Neander (1650-80),
   tr. C. Winkworth

265

1. Praise we now the Lord our God,
   all mankind in chorus;
   ceaselessly let seraphim,
   angels, pow'rs and cherubim
   sing with joy their praise of him,
   holy, Lord of Sabaoth.

2. All the earth and sea and sky,
   glorify their maker,
   blessed martyrs, prophets grand,
   Christ's beloved apostle-band,
   holy Church in every land.
   Sing his praise for ever.

3. Hail thou king of glory, Christ,
   born before all ages!
   Born of Mary, Virgin pure,
   thou didst us from death secure,
   opening wide to mankind poor,
   stores of heavenly treasure.

4. Seated now at God's right hand,
   bless thy chosen people;
   rule o'er us, dear Lord, we pray,
   keep us free from sin this day,
   save us, Lord, without delay,
   lest we be confounded.

5. In the solemn day of doom,
   we shall hear thy judgment;
   but remember, Lord, we cry,
   in that day when we shall die,
   how thy blood on us did lie,
   signing us thy people.

6. Praise we yet the Lord our God,
   throned in triune splendour:
   praise the Father, Lord of might,
   praise the Son, redeemer bright,
   praise the Spirit, source of light,
   through eternal ages.

D. McRoberts

266

1. Praise we our God with joy
   and gladness never ending;
   angels and saints with us
   their grateful voices blending.
   He is our Father dear,
   o'er filled with parent's love;
   mercies unsought, unknown,
   he showers from above.

2. He is our shepherd true;
   with watchful care unsleeping,
   on us, his erring sheep
   an eye of pity keeping;
   he with a mighty arm
   the bonds of sin doth break,
   and to our burden'd hearts
   in words of peace doth speak.

3. Graces in copious stream
   from that pure fount are welling,
   where, in our heart of hearts,
   our God hath set his dwelling.
   His word our lantern is;
   his peace our comfort still;
   his sweetness all our rest;
   our law, our life, his will.

Frederick Oakeley (1802-80) and others

267

1. Promised Lord, and Christ is he,
   may we soon his kingdom see.
   *Come, O Lord, quickly come,
   come in glory, come in glory,
   come in glory, quickly come.*

2. Teaching, healing once was he,
   may we soon his kingdom see.

3. Dead and buried once was he,
   may we soon his kingdom see.

4. Risen from the dead is he,
   may we soon his kingdom see.

5. Soon to come again is he,
   may we soon his kingdom see.
   *Come, O Lord, quickly come,
   in our lifetime, in our lifetime,
   in our lifetime may it be.*

*Roger Ruston,
based on a Jewish Passover Song*

268

1. Reap me the earth
      as a harvest to God,
   gather and bring it again,
   all that is his,
      to the Maker of all.
   Lift it and offer it high.
   *Bring bread, bring wine,
   give glory to the Lord;
   whose is the earth but God's,
   whose is the praise but his?*

2. Go with your song
      and your music with joy,
   go to the altar of God.
   Carry your offerings,
      fruits of the earth,
   work of your labouring hands.

3. Gladness and pity
      and passion and pain,
   all that is mortal in man,
   lay all before him,
      return him his gift,
   God, to whom all shall go home.

Peter Icarus

269

Rejoice in the Lord always,
and again I say rejoice.
Rejoice in the Lord always,
and again I say rejoice.
Rejoice, rejoice,
and again I say rejoice.
Rejoice, rejoice,
and again I say rejoice.

from Scripture

270

1. Rejoice! the Lord is King!
Your Lord and King adore;
mortals, give thanks and sing,
and triumph evermore:

Lift up your heart,
lift up your voice;
rejoice, again I say, rejoice.

2. Jesus the Saviour reigns,
the God of truth and love;
when he had purged our stains,
he took his seat above:

3. His kingdom cannot fail;
he rules o'er earth and heaven;
the keys of death and hell
are to our Jesus given:

4. He sits at God's right hand
till all his foes submit,
and bow to his command,
and fall beneath his feet:

Charles Wesley (1707-88)

271

1. Ride on! ride on in majesty!
Hark, all the tribes hosanna cry;
thy humble beast pursued his road
with palms and scattered garments
strowed.

2. Ride on! ride on in majesty!
In lowly pomp ride on to die;
O Christ, thy triumphs now begin
o'er captive death and conquered
sin.

3. Ride on! ride on in majesty!
The wingèd squadrons of the sky,
look down with sad and wondering
eyes
to see the approaching sacrifice.

4. Ride on! ride on in majesty!
Thy last and fiercest strife is nigh;
the Father, on his sapphire throne
expects his own anointed Son.

5. Ride on! ride on in majesty!
In lowly pomp ride on to die;
bow thy meek head to mortal pain,
then take, O God, thy power, and
reign.

H. H. Milman (1791-1868)

272

1. Round me falls the night,
Saviour be my light;
through the hours in darkness
shrouded
let me see thy face unclouded.
Let thy glory shine
in this heart of mine.

2. Earthly work is done,
earthly sounds are none;
rest in sleep and silence seeking,
let me hear thee softly speaking;
in my spirit's ear
whisper: "I am near".

3. Blessed heav'nly light
shining through earth's night;
voice that oft' of love has told me,
arms, so strong, to clasp and hold
me;
thou thy watch will keep,
Saviour o'er my sleep.

W. Romanis

273

1. Seasons come, seasons go,
   moon-struck tides will ebb and flow;
   when I forget my constant one
   he draws me back, he brings me
   home.

   O love, my love,
     I hear you far away.
   a distant storm
     that will refresh the day.

2. Seasons come, seasons go,
   petals fall though flowers grow;
   and when I doubt love lifts a hand
   and scatters stars like grains of sand.
   Oh love, my love,
     I see you passing by
   like birds that fearlessly
     possess the sky.

3. Seasons come, seasons go,
   times to reap and times to sow;
   but you are love, a fruitful vine,
   in ev'ry season yielding wine.
   I hear my love
     in laughter and in song,
   no day too short,
     no winter night too long.

   Michael Cockett

274

1. See, amid the winter's snow,
   born for us on earth below,
   see, the tender lamb appears,
   promised from eternal years.

   *Hail, thou ever-blessed morn,
   hail, redemption's happy dawn!
   Sing through all Jerusalem,
   Christ is born in Bethlehem.*

2. Lo, within a manger lies
   he who built the starry skies;
   he who, throned in heights sublime,
   sits amid the cherubim.

3. Say, ye holy shepherds, say,
   what your joyful news today?
   Wherefore have ye left your sheep
   on the lonely mountain steep?

4. 'As we watched at dead of night,
   lo, we saw a wondrous light;
   angels, singing peace on earth,
   told us of the Saviour's birth.'

5. Sacred infant, all divine,
   what a tender love was thine,
   thus to come from highest bliss,
   down to such a world as this!

6. Virgin mother, Mary blest,
   by the joys that fill thy breast,
   pray for us, that we may prove
   worthy of the Saviour's love.

   Edward Caswall (1814-78)

275

1. See us, Lord, about thine altar;
   though so many, we are one;
   many souls by love united
   in the heart of Christ thy Son.

2. Hear our prayers, O loving Father,
   hear in them thy Son, our Lord;
   hear him speak our love and worship,
   as we sing with one accord.

3. Once were seen the blood and water;
   now he seems but bread and wine;
   then in human form he suffered,
   now his form is but a sign.

4. Wheat and grape contain the
   meaning;
   food and drink he is to all;
   one in him, we kneel adoring,
   gathered by his loving call.

5. Hear us yet; so much is needful
   in our frail, disordered life;
   stay with us and tend our weakness
   till that day of no more strife.

6. Members of his mystic body
   now we know our prayer is heard,
   heard by thee, because thy children
   have received th' eternal word.

   John Greally

276

Shalom, my friend,
    shalom my friend, shalom, shalom,
the peace of Christ
    I give you today, shalom, shalom.

Sandra Joan Billington

277

1. Silent night, holy night,
  all is calm, all is bright,
  round yon virgin mother and child;
  holy infant so tender and mild:
  sleep in heavenly peace,
  sleep in heavenly peace.

2. Silent night, holy night.
  Shepherds quake at the sight,
  glories stream from heaven afar,
  heavenly hosts sing alleluia:
  Christ, the Saviour is born,
  Christ, the Saviour is born.

3. Silent night, holy night.
  Son of God, love's pure light
  radiant beams from thy holy face,
  with the dawn of redeeming grace:
  Jesus, Lord, at thy birth,
  Jesus, Lord, at thy birth.

Joseph Mohr (1792-1848),
tr. J. Young

278

Sing, my soul. Sing, my soul.
Sing, my soul, of his mercy.
Sing, my soul. Sing, my soul.
Sing, my soul, of his mercy.

1. The Lord is good to me.
  His light will shine on me.
  When city lights would blind my
                    eyes.
  He hears my silent call.
  His hands help when I fall.
  His gentle voice stills my sighs.

2. The Lord is good to me.
  His word will set me free
  when men would tie me to the
                 ground.

He mocks my foolish ways
with love that never fails.
When I'm most lost then I'm found.

3. The Lord is good to me.
  I hear him speak to me.
  His voice is in the rain that falls.
  He whispers in the air
  of his unending care.
  If I will hear, then he calls.

Michael Cockett

279

1. Sing, my tongue, the glorious battle,
  sing the last, the dread affray;
  o'er the cross, the victor's trophy,
  sound the high triumphal lay;
  how, the pains of death enduring,
  earth's redeemer won the day.

2. Faithful cross! above all other,
  one and only noble tree!
  None in foliage, none in blossom,
  none in fruit thy peer may be;
  sweetest wood and sweetest iron!
  Sweetest weight is hung on thee.

3. Bend, O lofty tree, thy branches,
  thy too rigid sinews bend;
  and awhile the stubborn hardness,
  which thy birth bestowed, suspend;
  and the limbs of heaven's high
                  monarch,
  gently on thine arms extend.

4. Thou alone wast counted worthy
  this world's ransom to sustain,
  that by thee a wrecked creation
  might its ark and haven gain,
  with the sacred blood anointed
  of the Lamb that hath been slain.

5. Praise and honour to the Father,
  praise and honour to the Son,
  praise and honour to the Spirit,
  ever three and ever one,
  one in might and one in glory,
  while eternal ages run.

Venantius Fortunatus (530-609),
tr. J. M. Neale

280

1. Sing of the bride
   and sing of the groom,
   and the wine that was flowing free,
   when the Lord was a guest
   at the wedding feast
   in a town in Galilee.

   Fill the pots with water
   and raise the glasses high,
   for the Lord has come to Cana
   and changed water into wine.

2. Sing of the bride
   and sing of the groom,
   and the feasting all night and day,
   with the wine running short
   at the wedding feast
   to the stewards' sad dismay.

3. "Please will you help,
   they have no more wine,"
   said a mother to her only son.
   He said: "Woman, don't you know
   you can't turn to me,
   for my time has not yet come."

4. "Wait till the day
   and wait till the time
   for the cross and for Calvary,
   but until that time
   here's a fine new wine
   with a taste that's fine and free."

5. Drink to the bride
   and drink to the groom
   at the wedding in Galilee,
   and drink to the life
   that is like new wine
   to all men who wish to be free.

   Michael Cockett

281

1. Sing of Mary, pure and lowly,
   virgin mother undefiled.
   Sing of God's own Son most holy,
   who became her little child.
   Fairest child of fairest mother,
   God, the Lord, who came to earth,
   Word made flesh, our very brother,
   takes our nature by his birth.

2. Sing of Jesus, son of Mary,
   in the home at Nazareth.
   Toil and labour cannot weary
   love enduring unto death.
   Constant was the love he gave her,
   though he went forth from her side,
   forth to preach and heal and suffer,
   till on Calvary he died.

3. Glory be to God the Father,
   glory be to God the Son;
   glory be to God the Spirit,
   glory to the three in one.
   From the heart of blessed Mary,
   from all saints the song ascends
   and the Church the strain re-echoes
   unto earth's remotest ends.

   Anonymous (c. 1914)

282

Sing, sing, sing, sing, sing, sing!
Sing! people of God, sing!
Sing with one accord.
Sing! people of God,
sing your praises to the Lord.

1. O Lord, how glorious over all
   the good earth is your name.
   You have exalted your majesty
   over ev'ry hill and plain.
   From the mouths of the little ones
   you fashion endless praise
   to silence all the vengeful ones
   and glorify your ways.

2. When we behold the heavens
   where your creation shines,
   the moon and stars you set in place
   to stand the test of time,
   what is man that you should mind,
   his sons that you should care?
   A little less than angels
   you have crowned him ev'rywhere.

3. You've given us dominion
   over all that you have made.
   We're masters of your handiwork
   and rule them unafraid.
   We're lords of the fish and birds,
   of beasts both wild and tame.
   O Lord, how glorious over all
   the good earth is your name.

   Sebastian Temple

283

1. Sing praises to God, sing praises,
   sing praises to God, sing praises,
   for he is the king of all the earth,
   sing praises to his name.

2. Give glory to God, give glory,
   give glory to God, give glory,
   for he is the king of all the earth,
   give glory to his name.

3. Give honour to God, give honour,
   give honour to God, give honour,
   for he is the king of all the earth,
   give honour to his name.

   Anonymous

284

1. Sing praises to the living God,
   glory, hallelujah.
   Come, adore the living God,
   glory, hallelujah.
   Though sun and moon may pass away
   his words will ever stay.
   His power is for evermore,
   glory, hallelujah.

   Glory to the Trinity.
   The undivided Unity,
   the Father, Son and Spirit one,
   from whom all life
   and greatness come.

2. And to the living God we sing,
   glory hallelujah.
   Let our love and praises ring,
   glory hallelujah.
   To all his sons he always gives
   his mercy and his love.
   So praise him now for evermore,
   glory hallelujah.

3. And to the God who cannot die,
   glory hallelujah.
   To the living God we cry,
   glory hallelujah.
   He promised to be with us and
   he lives in ev'ry one.
   We love him now for evermore,
   glory hallelujah.

   Sebastian Temple

285

1. Sleep, holy babe,
   upon thy mother's breast;
   great Lord of earth and sea and sky,
   how sweet it is to see thee lie
   in such a place of rest.

2. Sleep, holy babe;
   thine angels watch around,
   all bending low, with folded wings,
   before th'incarnate King of kings,
   in reverent awe profound.

3. Sleep, holy babe,
   while I with Mary gaze
   in joy upon that face awhile,
   upon the loving infant smile,
   which there divinely plays.

4. Sleep, holy babe,
   ah, take thy brief repose,
   too quickly will thy slumbers break,
   and thou to lengthen'd pains awake,
   that death alone shall close.

5. O lady blest,
   sweet Virgin, hear my cry;
   forgive the wrong that I have done
   to thee, in causing thy dear Son
   upon the cross to die.

   Edward Caswall (1814-78)

286

1. Songs of thankfulness and praise,
   Jesus, Lord to thee we raise,
   manifested by the star
   to the sages from afar;
   branch of royal David's stem,
   in thy birth at Bethlehem;
   anthems be to thee addressed;
   God in man made manifest.

2. Manifest at Jordan's stream,
   prophet, Priest and King supreme,
   and at Cana wedding-guest,
   in thy Godhead manifest,
   manifest in power divine,
   changing water into wine;
   anthems be to thee addressed;
   God in man made manifest.

3. Manifest in making whole,
   palsied limbs and fainting soul,
   manifest in valiant fight,
   quelling all the devil's might,
   manifest in gracious will,
   ever bringing good from ill;
   anthems be to thee addressed;
   God in man made manifest.

4. Sun and moon shall darkened be,
   stars shall fall, the heavens shall flee.
   Christ will then like lightning shine.
   All will see his glorious sign.
   All will see the judge appear;
   all will then the trumpet hear;
   thou by all wilt be confessed;
   God in man made manifest.

5. Grant us grace to see thee, Lord,
   mirrored in thy holy word;
   may we imitate thee now
   and be pure, as pure art thou;
   that we like to thee may be
   at thy great Epiphany,
   and may praise thee, ever blest,
   God in man made manifest.

Christopher Wordsworth (1807-85)

287

Sons of God, hear his holy Word!
Gather round the table of the Lord!
Eat his Body, drink his Blood,
and we'll sing a song of love.
Allelu, allelu, allelu, alleluia.

1. Brothers, sisters, we are one,
   and our life has just begun.
   In the Spirit we are young.
   We can live for ever.

2. Shout together to the Lord
   who has promised our reward:
   happiness a hundredfold,
   and we'll live forever.

3. Jesus gave a new command
   that we love our fellow man
   till we reach the promised land,
   where we'll live forever.

4. If we want to live with him;
   we must also die with him;
   die to selfishness and sin,
   and we'll rise forever.

5. Make the world a unity,
   make all men one family
   till we meet the Trinity
   and live with them forever.

6. With the Church we celebrate;
   Jesus' coming we await,
   so we make a holiday,
   so we'll live forever.

James Theim

288

1. Soul of my Saviour,
   sanctify my breast;
   Body of Christ,
   be thou my saving guest;
   Blood of my Saviour,
   bathe me in thy tide,
   wash me with water
   flowing from thy side.

2. Strength and protection
   may thy Passion be;
   O Blessed Jesus
   hear and answer me;
   deep in thy wounds, Lord,
   hide and shelter me;
   so shall I never,
   never part from thee.

3. Guard and defend me
   from the foe malign;
   in death's dread moments
   make me only thine;
   call me, and bid me
   come to thee on high,
   when I may praise thee
   with thy saints for aye.

Ascribed to John XXII (1249-1334),
tr. Anonymous

289

Spirit of the living God,
fall afresh on me.
Spirit of the living God,
fall afresh on me.
Break me, melt me,
mould me, fill me.
Spirit of the living God,
fall afresh on me.

Michael Iverson

290

1. Star of ocean, lead us;
   God for mother claims thee,
   ever Virgin names thee;
   gate of heaven, speed us.

2. Ave to thee crying
   Gabriel went before us;
   peace do thou restore us,
   Eva's knot untying.

3. Loose the bonds that chain us,
   darkened eyes enlighten,
   clouded prospects brighten,
   heavenly mercies gain us.

4. For thy sons thou carest;
   offer Christ our praying —
   still thy word obeying —
   whom on earth thou barest.

5. Purer, kinder maiden
   God did never fashion;
   pureness and compassion
   grant to hearts sin-laden.

6. From that sin release us,
   shield us, heavenward faring,
   heaven, that is but sharing
   in thy joy with Jesus.

7. Honour, praise and merit
   to our God address we;
   Three in One confess we,
   Father, Son and Spirit.

9th c., tr. R. A. Knox

291

Steal away, steal away,
steal away to Jesus.
Steal away, steal away home.
I ain't got long to stay here.

1. My Lord, he calls me.
   He calls me by the thunder.
   The trumpet sounds within my soul;
   I ain't got long to stay here.

2. Green trees are bending,
   the sinner stands a-trembling.
   The trumpet sounds within my soul;
   I ain't got long to stay here.

3. My Lord, he calls me,
   he calls me by the lightning.
   The trumpet sounds within my soul;
   I ain't got long to stay here.

Negro Spiritual

292

Suffer little children
to come unto me,
for theirs is the kingdom of heaven.
Suffer little children
to come unto me.
for theirs is the kingdom
of the Lord.

1. There came unto him
   children, little children,
   that he might lay his hands
   upon them,
   pray for and bless them,
   children, little children,
   gathered round our Lord.

2. The disciples said:
   "Children, little children,
   leave the Master to his prayer.
   Begone and stay not,
   children, little children,
   gathered round our Lord."

3. But Jesus said:
   "Children, little children,
   stay my blessing to receive.
   Forbid you not that
   children, little children,
   shall gather round the Lord."

4. "For you must be like
   children, little children,
   humble, simple, pure in heart.
   For it is to these
   children, little children,
   the kingdom of heav'n belongs."

Philip Green

293

1. Sweet heart of Jesus,
   fount of love and mercy,
   today we come,
   thy blessing to implore;
   O touch our hearts,
   so cold and so ungrateful,
   and make them, Lord,
   thine own for evermore.

   Sweet heart of Jesus, we implore,
   O make us love thee more and more.

2. Sweet heart of Jesus,
   make us know and love thee,
   unfold to us
   the treasures of thy grace;
   that so our hearts,
   from things of earth uplifted,
   may long alone
   to gaze upon thy face.

3. Sweet heart of Jesus,
   make us pure and gentle,
   and teach us how
   to do thy blessed will;
   to follow close
   the print of thy dear footsteps,
   and when we fall
   – sweet heart, oh, love us still.

4. Sweet heart of Jesus,
   bless all hearts that love thee,
   and may thine own
   heart ever blessed be,
   bless us, dear Lord,
   and bless the friends we cherish,
   and keep us true
   to Mary and to thee.

Traditional

294

1. Sweet sacrament divine,
   hid in thy earthly home,
   lo! round thy lowly shrine,
   with suppliant hearts we come;
   Jesus, to thee our voice we raise,
   in songs of love and heartfelt praise,
   sweet sacrament divine.

2. Sweet sacrament of peace,
   dear home of every heart,
   where restless yearnings cease,
   and sorrows all depart,
   there in thine ear all trustfully
   we tell our tale of misery,
   sweet sacrament of peace.

3. Sweet sacrament of rest,
   Ark from the ocean's roar,
   within thy shelter blest
   soon may we reach the shore,
   save us, for still the tempest raves;
   save, lest we sink beneath the waves
   sweet sacrament of rest.

4. Sweet sacrament divine,
   earth's light and jubilee,
   in thy far depths doth shine
   thy Godhead's majesty;
   sweet light, so shine on us, we pray,
   that earthly joys may fade away,
   sweet sacrament divine.

   Francis Stanfield (1835-1914)

295

1. Sweet Saviour, bless us ere we go,
   thy word into our minds instil;
   and make our lukewarm hearts to
   glow
   with lowly love and fervent will.

   Through life's long day
   and death's dark night,
   O gentle Jesus, be our light.

2. The day is done; its hours have run,
   and thou hast taken count of all,
   the scanty triumphs grace has won,
   the broken vow, the frequent fall.

3. Grant us, dear Lord, from evil ways,
   true absolution and release;
   and bless us more than in past days
   with purity and inward peace.

4. Do more than pardon; give us joy,
   sweet fear and sober liberty,
   and loving hearts without alloy,
   that only long to be like thee.

5. Labour is sweet, for thou hast toiled,
   and care is light, for thou hast cared;
   let not our works with self be soiled.
   Nor in unsimple ways ensnared.

6. For all we love – the poor, the sad,
   the sinful – unto thee we call;
   oh let thy mercy make us glad,
   thou art our Jesus and our all.

   Frederick William Faber (1814-63)

296

1. Take my hands
   and make them as your own,
   and use them for your
   Kingdom here on earth.
   Consecrate them to your care,
   anoint them for
   your service where
   you may need your gospel to be sown.

2. Take my hands.
   They speak now for my heart,
   and by their actions
   they will show their love.
   Guard them on their daily course,
   be their strength
   and guiding force
   to ever serve the Trinity above.

3. Take my hands.
   I give them to you, Lord.
   Prepare them for the
   service of your name.
   Open them to human need
   and by their love
   they'll sow your seed
   so all may know
   the love and hope you give.

   Sebastian Temple

297

Take our bread, we ask you,
take our hearts, we love you,
take our lives, oh Father,
we are yours, we are yours.

1. Yours as we stand
    at the table you set,
    yours as we eat the bread
    our hearts can't forget.
    We are the signs
    of your life with us yet;
    we are yours, we are yours.

2. Your holy people
    stand washed in your blood,
    Spirit filled, yet hungry,
    we await your food.
    Poor though we are,
    we have brought ourselves to you:
    we are yours, we are yours,

Joseph Wise

298

1. Thank you
    for giving me the morning.
    Thank you for ev'ry day that's new.
    Thank you
    that I can know my worries
    can be cast on you.

2. Thank you
    for all my friends and brothers.
    Thank you for all the men that live.
    Thank you
    for even greatest enemies
    I can forgive.

3. Thank you,
    I have my occupation.
    Thank you
    for ev'ry pleasure small.
    Thank you
    for music, light and gladness.
    Thank you for them all.

4. Thank you
    for many little sorrows.
    Thank you for ev'ry kindly word.
    Thank you
    for ev'rywhere your guidance
    reaches ev'ry land.

5. Thank you,
    I see your Word has meaning.
    Thank you, I know your Spirit here.
    Thank you
    because you love all people,
    those both far and near.

6. Thank you,
    O Lord, you spoke unto us.
    Thank you that for our words you care.
    Thank you,
    O Lord, you came among us,
    bread and wine to share.

7. Thank you,
    O Lord, your love is boundless.
    Thank you that I am full of you.
    Thank you,
    you made me feel so glad and
    thankful as I do.

Walter van der Haas
and Peter-Paul van Lelyveld

299

1. The bakerwoman
    in her humble lodge
    received a grain of wheat from God.
    For nine whole months
    the grain she stored.
    Behold the handmaid of the Lord.
    Make us the bread, Mary, Mary.
    Make us the bread,
    we need to be fed.

2. The bakerwoman took
    the road which led
    to Bethlehem, the house of bread.
    To knead the bread she laboured
    through the night,
    and brought it forth about midnight.
    Bake us the bread, Mary, Mary.
    Bake us the bread,
    we need to be fed.

3. She baked the bread for thirty years
   by the fire of her love
   and the salt of her tears,
   by the warmth of a heart
   so tender and bright,
   and the bread was golden
   brown and white.
   Bring us the bread, Mary, Mary.
   Bring us the bread,
   we need to be fed.
4. After thirty years
   the bread was done.
   It was taken to town
   by her only son;
   the soft white bread to be given free
   to the hungry people of Galilee.
   Give us the bread, Mary, Mary.
   Give us the bread,
   we need to be fed.
5. For thirty coins the bread was sold,
   and a thousand teeth so cold,
   so cold
   tore it to pieces on a Friday noon
   when the sun turned black
   and red the moon.
   Break us the bread, Mary, Mary.
   Break us the bread,
   we need to be fed.
6. And when she saw
   the bread so white,
   the living bread she had made
   at night,
   devoured as wolves might
   devour a sheep,
   the bakerwoman began to weep.
   Weep for the bread, Mary, Mary.
   Weep for the bread,
   we need to be fed.
7. But the bakerwoman's only son
   appeared to his friends
   when three days had run
   on the road which to Emmaus led,
   and they knew him in
   the breaking of bread.
   Lift up your head, Mary, Mary.
   Lift up your head,
   for now we've been fed.

Hubert Richards

300

1. The Church's one foundation,
   is Jesus Christ, her Lord;
   she is his new creation,
   by water and the Word;
   from heav'n he came and sought her
   to be his holy bride,
   with his own blood he bought her,
   and for her life he died.

2. Elect from every nation,
   yet one o'er all the earth,
   her charter of salvation
   one Lord, one faith, one birth;
   one holy name she blesses,
   partakes one holy food,
   and to one hope she presses,
   with every grace endued.

3. 'Mid toil, and tribulation,
   and tumult of her war,
   she waits the consummation
   of peace for evermore;
   till with the vision glorious
   her longing eyes are blest,
   and the great Church victorious
   shall be the Church at rest.

4. Yet she on earth hath union
   with God the Three in One,
   and mystic sweet communion
   with those whose rest is won:
   O happy ones and holy!
   Lord, give us grace that we
   like them, the meek and lowly
   on high may dwell with thee.

S. J. Stone (1830-1900)

301

1. The coming of our God
   our thoughts must now employ;
   then let us meet him on the road
   with songs of holy joy.

2. The co-eternal Son,
   a maiden's offspring see;
   a servant's form Christ putteth on,
   to set his people free.

3. Daughter of Sion, rise
to greet thine infant king,
nor let thy stubborn heart despise
the pardon he doth bring.

4. In glory from his throne
again will Christ descend,
and summon all that are his own
to joys that never end.

5. Let deeds of darkness fly
before the approaching morn,
for unto sin 'tis ours to die,
and serve the virgin-born.

6. Our joyful praises sing
to Christ, that set us free;
like tribute to the Father bring,
and, Holy Ghost, to thee.

Charles Coffin (1676-1749),
tr. R. Campbell

302

1. The day of resurrection!
Earth, tell it out abroad;
the Passover of gladness
the Passover of God!
From death to life eternal,
from earth unto the sky,
our Christ hath brought us over
with hymns of victory.

2. Our hearts be pure from evil,
that we may see aright
the Lord in rays eternal
of ressurection-light;
And listening to his accents,
may hear so calm and plain
his own 'All hail' and, hearing,
may raise the victor strain.

3. Now let the heavens be joyful,
and earth her song begin,
the round world keep high triumph,,
and all that is therein;
Let all things seen and unseen
their notes of gladness blend,
for Christ the Lord hath risen,
our joy that hath no end.

St. John Damascene (c. 750),
tr. J. M. Neale

303

1. The day thou gavest Lord, is ended:
the darkness falls at thy behest;
to thee our morning
hymns ascended;
thy praise shall sanctify our rest.

2. We thank thee that thy Church
unsleeping,
while earth rolls onward into light,
through all the world her
watch is keeping,
and rests not now by day or night.

3. As o'er each continent and island
the dawn leads on another day,
the voice of prayer is
never silent,
nor dies the strain of praise away.

4. The sun that bids us rest is waking
our brethren 'neath the western sky
and hour by hour fresh
lips are making
thy wondrous doings heard on high.

5. So be it, Lord; thy throne shall
never,
like earth's proud empire, pass away;
thy kingdom stands, and
grows for ever,
till all thy creatures own thy sway.

John Ellerton (1826-93)

304

1. The farmer in the fertile field is
sowing, sowing.
The seed is good,
the shoots of corn are
growing, growing, growing, growing.

2. An enemy with darnel seed is
sowing, sowing.
The weed that fights
the growing corn is
choking, choking, choking, choking.

3. Together till the harvest they'll be
growing, growing.
But then what has
been sown we will be
reaping, reaping, reaping, reaping.

4. The corn is taken to the barn for
storing, storing.
The weed is cast
into the fire for
burning, burning, burning, burning.

Michael Cockett

305

1. The first Nowell the angel did say
was to certain poor shepherds in
fields as they lay:
in fields where they lay keeping
their sheep,
on a cold winter's night that was
so deep.

*Nowell, Nowell, Nowell, Nowell,
born is the King of Israel!*

2. They lookèd up and saw a star,
shining in the east, beyond them
far,
and to the earth it gave great light,
and so it continued both day and
night.

3. And by the light of that same star,
three wise men came from country
far.
To seek for a king was their intent,
and to follow the star wherever it
went.

4. This star drew nigh to the north-
west,
o'er Bethlehem it took its rest,
and there it did both stop and stay
right over the place where Jesus lay

5. Then entered in those wise men
three,
full reverently upon their knee,
and offered there in his presence,
their gold and myrrh and
frankincense.

6. Then let us all with one accord
sing praises to our heavenly Lord,
that hath made heaven and earth of
nought,
and with his blood mankind hath
bought.

Traditional Old English

306

1. The God whom earth,
and sea, and sky,
adore and laud and magnify,
who o'er their threefold fabric
reigns,
the Virgin's spotless womb contains.

2. The God whose will
by moon and sun,
and all things in due course is done,
is borne upon a maiden's breast
by fullest heavenly grace possessed.

3. How blest that mother,
in whose shrine
the great Artificer divine,
whose hand contains the earth and
sky,
vouchsafed, as in his ark, to lie!

4. Blest, in the message Gabriel brought;
blest, by the work the Spirit wrought;
from whom the great desire of earth,
took human flesh and human birth.

5. All honour, laud and glory be,
O Jesus, virgin-born, to thee!
All glory, as is ever meet
to Father and to Paraclete.

*Ascribed to Venantius Fortunatus
(530-609), tr. J. M. Neale*

307

1. The green life rises from the earth,
the life of sun and rain and soil,
in seed and shoot, in grain and grape,
in food and drink for men.

   *Praise be to God for all his gifts,
   praise for the bread and wine.*

2. The Lord of Spring, the Lord of Life,
made bread his body, wine his blood.
The life of earth, the life of God,
becomes the life of man.

3. We take in hand the bread and wine,
reminder of the dying Lord.
This food, this drink, this feast of joy
gives Christ's own life to us.

4. "The Son of Man must die," said he,
"my death will raise you all to life.
No blade is born, no harvest reaped,
until the seed has died.

5. "These are the signs of death and life,
the bread you break, the cup you share:
my dying gift in which I live,
my death is life to you."

6. Give praise to God who gave this gift,
his very Son, to bring us life.
The Father's life in him is ours,
his Spirit breathes in us.

Luke Connaughton

308

1. The head that once was crowned
with thorns
is crowned with glory now:
a royal diadem adorns
the mighty victor's brow.

2. The highest place that heaven
affords
is his, is his by right.
The King of kings and Lord of lords,
and heaven's eternal light;

3. The joy of all who dwell above,
the joy of all below,
to whom he manifests his love,
and grants his name to know.

4. To them the cross, with all its shame
with all its grace is given;
their name an everlasting name,
their joy the joy of heaven.

5. They suffer with their Lord below,
they reign with him above,
their profit and their joy to know
the mystery of his love.

6. The cross he bore is life and health,
though shame and death to him;
his people's hope, his people's
wealth,
their everlasting theme.

Thomas Kelly (1769-1854)

309

1. The heav'nly Word, proceeding forth
yet leaving not the Father's side,
accomplishing his work on earth
had reached at length life's eventide.

2. By false disciple to be giv'n
to foemen for his life athirst,
himself, the very bread of heav'n,
he gave to his disciples first.

3. He gave himself in either kind,
   he gave his flesh, he gave his blood;
   in love's own fullness thus designed,
   of the whole man to be the food.

4. O saving victim, opening wide
   the gate of heav'n to man below,
   our foes press on from every side;
   thine aid supply, thy strength
                                bestow.

5. To thy great name be endless praise,
   Immortal Godhead, one in three;
   O grant us endless length of days
   in our true native land with thee.

   St. Thomas Aquinas (1227-74),
   tr. J. M. Neale

310

The King of glory comes
the nation rejoices
open the gates before him,
lift up your voices.

1. Who is the King of glory
   how shall we call him?
   He is Emmanuel,
   the promised of ages.

2. In all of Galilee,
   in city and village,
   he goes among his people,
   curing their illness.

3. Sing then of David's Son,
   our Saviour and brother;
   in all of Galilee
   was never another.

4. He gave his life for us,
   the pledge of salvation.
   He took upon himself
   the sins of the nation.

5. He conquered sin and death;
   he truly has risen.
   And he will share with us
   his heavenly vision.

   W. F. Jabusch

311

1. The King of love my Shepherd is,
   whose goodness faileth never;
   I nothing lack if I am his
   and he is mine for ever.

2. Where streams of living water flow
   my ransomed soul he leadeth,
   and where the verdant pastures grow
   with food celestial feedeth.

3. Perverse and foolish oft I strayed
   but yet in love he sought me,
   and on his shoulder gently laid,
   and home, rejoicing, brought me.

4. In death's dark vale I fear no ill
   with thee, dear Lord, beside me;
   thy rod and staff my comfort still,
   thy cross before to guide me.

5. Thou spread'st a table in my sight,
   thy unction grace bestoweth:
   and O what transport of delight
   from thy pure chalice floweth!

6. And so through all the length of
                                days
   thy goodness faileth never;
   good Shepherd, may I sing thy praise
   within thy house for ever.

   Henry Williams Baker (1821-77)

312

1. The Lord's my shepherd, I'll not
                                want,
   he makes me down to lie
   in pastures green. He leadeth me
   the quiet waters by.

2. My soul he doth restore again,
   and me to walk doth make
   within the paths of righteousness,
   e'en for his own name's sake.

3. Yea, though I walk in death's dark
                                      vale,
   yet will I fear none ill.
   For thou art with me, and thy rod
   and staff me comfort still.

4. My table thou hast furnishèd
   in presence of my foes,
   my head thou dost with oil anoint,
   and my cup overflows.

5. Goodness and mercy all my life
   shall surely follow me.
   And in God's house for evermore
   my dwelling-place shall be.

Paraphrased from Ps. 22(23)
in the "Scottish Psalter" 1650

313

1. The Mass is ended, all go in peace.
   We must diminish,
       and Christ increase.
   We take him with us
       where'er we go
   that through our actions
       his life may show.

2. We witness his love to ev'ryone
   by our communion
       with Christ the Son.
   We take the Mass to
       where men may be,
   so Christ may shine forth
       for all to see.

3. Thanks to the Father
       who shows the way.
   His life within us
       throughout each day.
   Let all our living
       and loving be
   to praise and honour
       the Trinity.

4. The Mass is ended, all go in peace.
   We must diminish
       and Christ increase.
   We take him with us
       where'er we go
   that through our actions
       his life may show.

Sebastian Temple

314

1. The prophet in his hunger
       asked for bread.
   He asked the poor
       and famine was their guest.
   They saw starvation
       walking in the street,
   the doomed who thought
       to eat their last and die.

2. It is the Lord
       who lights the blinded eye,
   who lends the poor his wealth,
       the weak his strength,
   who feeds us with
       his everlasting love,
   and pours for men
       his justice like strong wine.

3. Because the widow
       offered of her last,
   and opened to his need
       her empty hand,
   Elijah promised her:
       "You shall not want.
   Your larder never shall
       be clean of food."

4. The widow and the orphan
       are his care;
   whom none will else defend,
       he will defend:
   he puts the strutting pride
       of tyrants down,
   and raises up the lowly
       from the dust.

5. See, in the temple,
       how with gestures wide,
   the rich men cast
       their casual gold to God,
   the widow offers
       all her dwindling purse,
   the pence of poverty —
       a richer gift.

Luke Connaughton

315

1. The race that long in darkness pined
   has seen a glorious light:
   the people dwell in day, who dwelt
   in death's surrounding night.

2. To hail thy rise, thou better sun,
   the gathering nations come,
   joyous as when the reapers bear
   the harvest treasures home.

3. To us a child of hope is born,
   to us a Son is given;
   him shall the tribes of earth obey,
   him all the hosts of heaven.

4. His name shall be the Prince of Peace
   for evermore adored,
   the Wonderful, the Counsellor,
   the great and mighty Lord.

5. His power increasing still shall
                               spread,
   his reign no end shall know;
   justice shall guard his throne above,
   and peace abound below.

   John Morison (1749-98)

316

1. There is a green hill far away,
   without a city wall,
   where the dear Lord was crucified
   who died to save us all.

2. We may not know, we cannot tell,
   what pains he had to bear,
   but we believe it was for us
   he hung and suffered there.

3. He died that we might be forgiven,
   he died to make us good;
   that we might go at last to heaven,
   saved by his precious blood.

4. There was no other good enough
   to pay the price of sin;
   he only could unlock the gate
   of heaven, and let us in.

5. O, dearly, dearly has he loved,
   and we must love him too,
   and trust in his redeeming blood,
   and try his works to do.

   Cecil Frances Alexander (1818-95)

317

1. There is a world
       where people come and go
   about their ways and
       never care to know
   that ev'ry step
       they take is placed on roads
   made out of men
       who had to carry loads too hard
       to bear.

   "That world's not ours,"
       that's what we always say.
   "We'll build a new one
       but some other day."
   When will we wake
       from comfort and from ease,
   and strive together
       to create a world of love and peace?

2. There is a world
       where people walk alone,
   and have around them
       men with hearts of stone,
   who would not spare
       one second of their day,
   or spend their breath
       in order just to say: "Your pain
       is mine."

3. There is a world
       where brothers cannot meet
   with one another
       where the tramp of feet
   brings men of ice,
       men who would force apart
   friends of all races
       having but one heart, a heart of
       love.

   Estelle White

318

1. The royal banners forward go,
   the cross shines forth in mystic glow,
   where he in flesh, our flesh who
   made,
   our sentence bore, our ransom paid.

2. There whilst he hung, his sacred side
   by soldier's spear was open'd wide,
   to cleanse us in the precious flood
   of water mingled with his blood.

3. Fulfill'd is now what David told
   in true prophetic song of old,
   how God the heathen's king should
   be;
   for God is reigning from the tree.

4. O tree of glory, tree most fair,
   ordain'd those holy limbs to bear,
   how bright in purple robe it stood,
   the purple of a saviour's blood!

5. Upon its arms, like balance true,
   he weigh'd the price for sinners due,
   the price which none but he could
   pay:
   and spoil'd the spoiler of his prey.

6. To thee, eternal Three in One,
   let homage meet by all be done,
   as by the cross thou dost restore,
   so rule and guide us evermore.

   Venantius Fortunatus (530-609),
   tr. J. M. Neale and others

319

1. The Spirit of the Lord
      is now upon me
   to heal the broken heart
      and set the captives free,
   to open prison doors
      and make the blind to see.
   The Spirit of the Lord
      is now on me.

   Anonymous

320

1. The tree of life grows in Paradise,
   and its roots reach out ev'rywhere:
   to the North, to the South,
      to the East and West
   and all its branches
      praise the living God!

2. The fire of life burns in Paradise,
   and its flames reach out ev'rywhere:
   to the North, to the South,
      to the East and West,
   its warmth and light shall
      praise the living God!

3. The book of life is read in Paradise,
   and its name's called out ev'rywhere:
   to the North, to the South,
      to the East and West,
   and all its pages
      praise the living God!

4. The Lord of life lives in Paradise,
   and his arms reach out ev'rywhere:
   to the North, to the South,
      to the East and West,
   and all his friends shall
      praise the living God!

   James Thiem

321

1. The Virgin Mary had a baby boy,
   the Virgin Mary had a baby boy,
   the Virgin Mary had a baby boy,
   and they said that his name was
   Jesus.

   He came from the glory,
   he came from the glorious kingdom.
   He came from the glory,
   he came from the glorious kingdom.
   Oh yes, believer,
   Oh yes, believer.
   He came from the glory,
   he came from the glorious kingdom.

2. The angels sang
   when the baby was born . . .
   and proclaimed him
   the Saviour Jesus.

3. The wise men saw
   where the baby was born . . .
   and they saw
   that his name was Jesus.

   Traditional West Indian

322

1. The wandering flock of Israel
   is scattered and far
   from home and hope;
   the Shepherd alone,
   with crook and staff,
   can find them and lead
   and keep them safe.

   He made and upheld us,
   granted grace;
   his smile is our peace,
   his word our hope.

2. I walk on the heights,
   I climb and cling,
   the terror beneath,
   the ice aloft.
   I look for his tracks,
   await his hand
   to help and to hold,
   to guide and save.

3. I thirst for his word
   as grass in drought,
   dry, brittle and barren,
   parched and brown;
   no shower can fall,
   no sap rise green
   no hope, if the Lord
   should send no rain.

4. Creator of all,
   your craftman's care
   with fashioning hand
   caressed our clay:
   this vine is the work
   your hands have wrought,
   your love is the sun,
   our soil of growth.

   J. Smith

323

1. They hung him on a cross,
   they hung him on a cross,
   they hung him on a cross for me.
   One day when I was lost,
   they hung him on a cross,
   they hung him on a cross for me.

2. They whipped him up the hill, . . .

3. They speared him in the side, . . .

4. The blood came streaming down . . .

5. He hung his head and died, . . .

6. He's coming back again, . . .

   Spiritual

324

1. They say I am wise
    and they say I am King.
   I'm a carpenter's son
    and I don't own a thing.
   They say I am rich
    and they say I am poor,
   and when I came knocking
    they bolted the door.

2. They asked me for bread
    and they asked for a sign.
   I gave them some bread
    and I gave them some wine.
   The bread was my body,
    the wine was my blood.
   They still turned away from me
    looking for food.

3. They shouted with joy.
    They laid palms on the road,
   but into the town
    on a donkey I rode.
   They said: "Do not go
    for we can't stand the loss."
   The very next morning
    they gave me a cross.

4. They brought me down low
    though they hung me up high.
   They brought me to life
    though they left me to die.
   They buried me deep
    with a stone at my head,
   but I am the living
    and they are the dead.

Michael Cockett

325

1. This day God gives me
   strength of high heaven,
   sun and moon shining,
    flame in my hearth,
   flashing of lightning,
   wind in its swiftness,
   deeps of the ocean,
    firmness of earth.

2. This day God sends me
   strength as my steersman,
   might to uphold me,
    wisdom as guide.
   Your eyes are watchful,
   your ears are listening,
   your lips are speaking,
    friend at my side.

3. God's way is my way,
   God's shield is round me,
   God's host defends me,
    saving from ill.
   Angels of heaven,
   drive from me always
   all that would harm me,
    stand by me still.

4. Rising, I thank you,
   mighty and strong One,
   King of creation,
    giver of rest,
   firmly confessing
   Threeness of Persons,
   Oneness of Godhead,
    Trinity blest.

Adapted from St. Patrick's Breastplate

James Quinn, S.J.

326

1. This is the image of the queen
   who reigns in bliss above;
   of her who is the hope of men,
   whom men and angels love.
   Most holy Mary, at thy feet
   I bend a suppliant knee;
   in this thy own sweet month of May,
   do thou remember me.

2. The homage offered at the feet
   of Mary's image here
   to Mary's self at once ascends
   above the starry sphere.
   Most holy Mary, at thy feet
   I bend a suppliant knee;
   in all my joy, in all my pain,
   do thou remember me.

3. How fair soever be the form
   which here your eyes behold,
   its beauty is by Mary's self
   excell'd a thousandfold.
   Most holy Mary, at thy feet,
   I bend a suppliant knee;
   in my temptations each and all,
   do thou remember me.

4. Sweet are the flow'rets we have
   culled,
   this image to adorn;
   but sweeter far is Mary's self,
   that rose without a thorn.
   Most holy Mary, at thy feet
   I bend a suppliant knee;
   when on the bed of death I lie,
   do thou remember me.

5. O lady, by the stars that make
   a glory round thy head;
   and by the pure uplifted hands,
   that for thy children plead;
   when at the judgment-seat I stand,
   and my dread saviour see;
   when waves of night around me roll
   O then remember me.

Edward Caswall (1814-78)

327

1. This is my will,
   my one command,
   that love should dwell
   among you all.
   This my will
   that you should love
   as I have shown
   that I love you.

2. No greater love
   a man can have
   than that he die
   to save his friends.
   You are my friends
   if you obey
   all I command
   that you should do.

3. I call you now
   no longer slaves;
   no slave knows all
   his master does.
   I call you friends,
   for all I hear
   my Father say
   you hear from me.

4. You chose not me,
   but I chose you,
   that you should go
   and bear much fruit.
   I called you out
   that you in me
   should bear much fruit
   that will abide.

5. All that you ask
   my Father dear
   for my name's sake
   you shall receive.
   This is my will,
   my one command,
   that love should dwell
   in each, in all.

James Quinn S.J.

328

1. This joyful Eastertide,
   away with sin and sorrow,
   my love, the Crucified,
   hath sprung to life this morrow:

   Had Christ, that once was slain,
   ne'er burst his three-day prison,
   our faith had been in vain:
   but now hath Christ arisen.

2. My flesh in hope shall rest,
   and for a season slumber:
   till trump from east to west
   shall wake the dead in number:

3. Death's flood hath lost his chill,
   since Jesus crossed the river:
   lover of souls, from ill
   my passing soul deliver:

   George Ratclife Woodward
   (1849-1934)

329

This little light of mine,
I'm gonna let it shine.
This little light of mine,
I'm gonna let it shine.
This little light of mine,
I'm gonna let it shine,
let it shine, let it shine, let it shine.

1. The light that shines
   is the light of love,
   lights the darkness from above.
   It shines on me
   and it shines on you,
   and shows what the
   power of love can do.
   I'm gonna shine my light
   both far and near,
   I'm gonna shine my light
   both bright and clear.
   Where there's a dark corner
   in this land
   I'm gonna let my little light shine.

2. On Monday he
   gave me the gift of love,
   Tuesday peace came from above.
   On Wednesday he
   told me to have more faith,
   on Thursday he
   gave me a little more grace.
   Friday he told me just to
   watch and pray,
   Saturday he told me just
   what to say.
   On Sunday he gave me
   the power divine
   to let my little light shine.

   Traditional

330

1. Thou wilt keep him in perfect peace,
   thou wilt keep him in perfect peace,
   thou wilt keep him in perfect peace
   whose mind is stayed on thee.

2. Marvel not, I say unto you,
   marvel not, I say unto you,
   marvel not, I say unto you,
   you must be born again.

3. Though your sins as scarlet be,
   though your sins as scarlet be,
   though your sins as scarlet be,
   they shall be white as snow.

4. If the Son shall set you free,
   if the Son shall set you free,
   if the Son shall set you free,
   you shall be free indeed.

   Anonymous

331

1. Thy hand, O God, has guided
thy flock from age to age;
the wondrous tale is written,
full clear, on ev'ry page;
our fathers owned thy goodness,
and we their deeds record;
and both of this bear witness:
one Church, one Faith, one Lord.

2. Thy heralds brought glad tidings
to greatest, as to least;
they bade men rise, and hasten
to share the great king's feast;
and this was all their teaching,
in every deed and word,
to all alike proclaiming
one Church, one Faith, one Lord.

3. When shadows thick were falling,
and all seemed sunk in night,
thou, Lord, didst send thy servants,
thy chosen sons of light.
On them and on thy people
thy plenteous grace was poured,
and this was still their message:
one Church, one Faith, one Lord.

4. Through many a day of darkness,
through many a scene of strife,
the faithful few fought bravely,
to guard the nation's life.
Their gospel of redemption,
sin pardoned, man restored,
was all in this enfolded:
one Church, one Faith, one Lord.

5. And we, shall we be faithless?
Shall hearts fail, hands hang down?
Shall we evade the conflict,
and cast away our crown?
Not so: in God's deep counsels
some better thing is stored;
we will maintain, unflinching,
one Church, one Faith, one Lord.

6. Thy mercy will not fail us,
nor leave thy work undone;
with thy right hand to help us
the vict'ry shall be won;
and then, by men and angels
thy name shall be adored.
And this shall be their anthem:
one Church, one Faith, one Lord.

E. H. Plumptre (1821-91)

332

1. To Christ the Lord of worlds we
sing,
the nations' universal king.
Hail, conqu'ring Christ, whose reign
alone
over our hearts and souls we own.

2. Christ, who art known the prince of
peace,
bid all rebellious tumults cease;
call home thy straying sheep, and
hold
for ever in one faithful fold.

3. For this, thine arms, on Calvary,
were stretched across th' empurpled
tree,
and the sharp spear that through
thee ran
laid bare the heart that burned for
man.

4. For this, in forms of bread and wine
lies hid the plenitude divine,
and from thy wounded body runs
the stream of life to all thy sons.

5. May those who rule o'er men below
thee for their greater sovereign
know,
and human wisdom, arts, and laws,
in thee repose as in their cause.

6. Let kingly signs of pomp and state
   unto thy name be dedicate,
   city and hearth and household be
   under thy gentle sceptre free.

7. Praise be to Christ, whose name and
                                throne
   o'er every throne and name we own;
   and equal praises still repeat
   the Father and the Paraclete.

   Roman Breviary, tr. W. H. Shewring

333

1. To Christ, the Prince of peace,
   and Son of God most high,
   the father of the world to come,
   sing we with holy joy.

2. Deep in his heart for us
   the wound of love he bore;
   that love wherewith he still inflames
   the hearts that him adore.

3. O Jesu, victim blest,
   what else but love divine
   could thee constrain to open thus
   that sacred heart of thine?

4. O fount of endless life,
   O spring of water clear,
   O flame celestial, cleansing all
   who unto thee draw near!

5. Hide us in thy dear heart,
   for thither we do fly;
   there seek thy grace through life, in
                                death
   thine immortality.

6. Praise to the Father be,
   and sole-begotten Son;
   praise, holy Paraclete, to thee
   while endless ages run.

   Catholicum Hymnologium
   Germanicum (1587) tr. E. Caswall

334

1. To Jesus' Heart, all burning
   with fervent love for men,
   my heart with fondest yearning
   shall raise its joyful strain.
   While ages course along,
   blest be with loudest song
   the sacred heart of Jesus
   by ev'ry heart and tongue.
   The sacred heart of Jesus
   by ev'ry heart and tongue.

2. O Heart, for me on fire
   with love no man can speak,
   my yet untold desire
   God gives me for thy sake.

3. Too true, I have forsaken
   thy love for wilful sin;
   yet now let me be taken
   back by thy grace again.

4. As thou are meek and lowly,
   and ever pure of heart,
   so may my heart be wholly
   of thine the counterpart.

5. When life away is flying,
   and earth's false glare is done;
   still, sacred Heart, in dying
   I'll say I'm all thine own.

   Aloys Schlor (1805-52),
   tr. A. J. Christie

335

1. To the name that brings salvation
   honour, worship, laud we pay:
   that for many a generation
   hid in God's foreknowledge lay;
   but to ev'ry tongue and nation
   Holy Church proclaims today.

2. Name of gladness, name of pleasure,
   by the tongue ineffable,
   name of sweetness passing measure,
   to the ear delectable;
   'tis our safeguard and our treasure,
   'tis our help 'gainst sin and hell.

3. 'Tis the name of adoration,
   'tis the name of victory;
   'tis the name for meditation
   in the vale of misery;
   'tis the name for veneration
   by the citizens on high.

4. 'Tis the name by right exalted
   over every other name:
   that when we are sore assaulted
   puts our enemies to shame:
   strength to them that else had
   halted,
   eyes to blind, and feet to lame.

5. Jesu, we thy name adoring,
   long to see thee as thou art:
   of thy clemency imploring
   so to write it in our heart,
   that hereafter, upward soaring,
   we with angels may have part.

15th c., tr. J. M. Neale

336

1. Trust is in the eyes
      of a tiny babe
   leaning on his mother's breast.
   In the eager beat
      of a young bird's wings
   on the day it leaves the nest.

It is the living Spirit
filling the earth, bringing to birth
a world of love and laughter,
joy in the light of the Lord.

2. Hope is in the rain
      that makes crystal streams
   tumble down a mountain side,
   and in every man
      who repairs his nets,
   waiting for the rising tide.

3. Love is in the hearts
      of all those who seek
   freedom for the human race.
   Love is in the touch
      of the hand that heals,
   and the smile that lights a face.

4. Strength is in the wind
      as it bends the trees,
   warmth is in the bright red flame,
   light is in the sun
      and the candle-glow,
   cleansing are the ocean's waves.

337 *Estelle White*

1. Unto us is born a Son,
   King of quires supernal:
   see on earth his life begun,
   of lords the Lord eternal,
   of lords the Lord eternal.

2. Christ, from heav'n descending low,
   comes on earth a stranger:
   ox and ass their owner know
   becradled in a manger,
   becradled in a manger.

3. This did Herod sore affray,
   and grievously bewilder:
   so he gave the word to slay,
   and slew the little childer,
   and slew the little childer.

4. Of his love and mercy mild
   this the Christmas story,
   and O that Mary's gentle Child
   might lead us up to glory!
   Might lead us up to glory!

5. O and A and A and O
   cum cantibus in choro,
   let the merry organ go,
   Benedicamus Domino,
   Benedicamus Domino.

15th c., tr. G. R. Woodward

338

1. Vaster far than any ocean,
   deeper than the deepest sea
   is the love of Christ my Saviour,
   reaching through eternity.

2. But my sins are truly many,
   is God's grace so vast, so deep?
   Yes, there's grace o'er sin
                    abounding,
   grace to pardon, grace to keep.

3. Can he quench my thirst for ever?
   Will his Spirit strength impart?
   Yes, he gives me living water
   springing up within my heart.

Author unknown

339

1. Virgin, wholly marvellous,
   who didst bear God's Son for us,
   worthless is my tongue and weak
   of thy purity to speak.

2. Who can praise thee as he ought?
   Gifts, with every blessing fraught,
   gifts that bring the gifted life,
   thou didst grant us, Maiden-Wife.

3. God became thy lowly Son,
   made himself thy little one,
   raising men to tell thy worth
   high in heav'n as here on earth.

4. Heav'n and earth, and all that is
   thrill today with ecstasies,
   chanting glory unto thee,
   singing praise with festal glee.

5. Cherubim with fourfold face,
   are no peers of thine in grace;
   and the six-wing'd seraphim
   shine, amid thy splendour, dim.

6. Purer art thou than are all
   heav'nly hosts angelical,
   who delight with pomp and state
   on thy beauteous Child to wait.

St. Ephrem Syrus (c. 307-373),
tr. J. W. Atkinson

340

Walk with me, oh my Lord,
through the darkest night
*   and brightest day.*
Be at my side, oh Lord,
hold my hand
*   and guide me on my way.*

1. Sometimes the road seems long,
   my energy is spent.
   Then, Lord, I think of you
   and I am given strength.

2. Stones often bar my path
   and there are times I fall,
   but you are always there
   to help me when I call.

3. Just as you calmed the wind
   and walked upon the sea,
   conquer, my living Lord,
   the storms that threaten me.

4. Help me to pierce the mists
   that cloud my heart and mind
   so that I shall not fear
   the steepest mountain-side.

5. As once you healed the lame
   and gave sight to the blind,
   help me when I'm downcast
   to hold my head up high.

Estelle White

341

1. We are gathering together unto him.
   We are gathering together unto him.
   Unto him shall the gath'ring
   of the people be.
   We are gathering together unto him.

2. We are offering together unto him.
   We are offering together unto him.
   Unto him shall the offering
   of the people be.
   We are offering together unto him.

3. We are singing together unto him.
   We are singing together unto him.
   Unto him shall the singing
   of the people be.
   We are singing together unto him.

4. We are praying together unto him.
   We are praying together unto him.
   Unto him shall the praying
   of the people be.
   We are praying together unto him.

   Anonymous

342

1. We are one in the Spirit,
   we are one in the Lord,
   we are one in the Spirit
   we are one in the Lord,
   and we pray that all unity
   may one day be restored.

   *And they'll know we are Christians
   by our love, by our love,
   yes, they'll know we are Christians
   by our love.*

2. We will walk with each other,
   we will walk hand in hand.
   We will walk with each other,
   we will walk hand in hand.
   And together we'll spread the news
   that God is in our land.

3. We will work with each other,
   we will work side by side.
   We will work with each other,
   we will work side by side.
   And we'll guard each man's dignity
   and save each man's pride.

4. All praise to the Father
   from whom all things come,
   and all praise to Christ Jesus,
   his only Son,
   and all praise to the Spirit
   who makes us one.

   Peter Scholtes

343

1. We bring our gifts to the Lord,
   our God.
   We bring our gifts to the Lord,
   our God.

2. We bring our love to the Lord,
   our God.
   We bring our love to the Lord,
   our God.

3. We bring ourselves to the Lord,
   our God.
   We bring ourselves to the Lord,
   our God.

   Estelle White

344

1. We celebrate this festive day
   with pray'r and joyful song.
   Our Father's house is home to us,
   we know that we belong.

   *The bread is broken, wine is poured,
   a feast to lift us up!
   Then thank the Lord who gives
                        himself
   as food and saving cup!*

2. The door is open, enter in
   and take your place by right.
   For you've been chosen as his guest
   to share his love and light.

3. We come together as the twelve
   came to the Upper Room.
   Our host is Jesus Christ the Lord,
   now risen from the tomb.

4. Who travels needs both food and
                                    drink
   to help him on his way.
   Refreshed and strong we'll journey
                                    on
   and face another day.

5. Who shares this meal receives the
                                    Lord
   who lives, though he was dead.
   So death can hold no terrors now
   for those who eat this bread.

                    Willard F. Jabusch

345

1. We gather together
   as brothers and sisters
   for Jesus our Lord truly lives.
   He's risen in glory;
   the full gospel story,
   what freedom and courage it gives.

   He binds up the wounded
   and the broken.
   He gives the poor his chalice
   and his bread.
   The Father has raised him,
   together we'll praise him,
   and march with the Lord
   at our head.

2. For mother and father,
   for sister and brother,
   for children and husband and wife,
   his Word spreads like flame,
   for all people came,
   bringing peace and the seeds of new
                                    life.

3. God takes what is foolish,
   he chooses the weakest
   to put wise and strong both to
                                    shame.
   Give thanks to the Father,
   we live in Christ Jesus,
   bow low and sing sweetly his name.

                    Willard F. Jabusch

346

1. We plough the fields and scatter
   the good seed on the land,
   but it is fed and watered
   by God's almighty hand;
   he sends the snow in winter,
   the warmth to swell the grain,
   the breezes and the sunshine,
   and soft refreshing rain.

   All good gifts around us
   are sent from heav'n above,
   then thank the Lord,
   O thank the Lord for all his love.

2. He only is the maker
   of all things near and far;
   he paints the wayside flower,
   he lights the ev'ning star.
   The winds and waves obey him,
   by him the birds are fed:
   much more to us his children,
   he gives our daily bread.

3. We thank thee then, O Father,
   for all things bright and good:
   the seed-time and the harvest,
   our life, our health, our food.
   No gifts have we to offer
   for all thy love imparts,
   but that which thou desirest,
   our humble, thankful hearts.

                    M. Claudius (1740-1815),
                    tr. J. M. Campbell

347

1. Were you there
   when they crucified my Lord?
   Were you there
   when they crucified my Lord?
   Oh sometimes it causes me
   to tremble, tremble, tremble.
   Were you there
   when they crucified my Lord?

2. Were you there
   when they nailed him to a tree? . . .

3. Were you there
   when they pierced him in the side?

4. Were you there
   when the sun refused to shine? . . .

5. Were you there
   when they laid him in the tomb? . .

6. Were you there
   when he rose from out the tomb? .

Negro Spiritual

348

1. We shall overcome,
   we shall overcome,
   we shall overcome some day.
   Oh, deep in my heart I do believe
   that we shall overcome some day.

2. We'll walk hand in hand . . .

3. We shall live in peace . . .

4. We shall live with him . . .

Traditional

349

1. We three Kings of Orient are;
   bearing gifts we traverse afar,
   field and fountain, moor and
               mountain,
   following yonder star.

   O Star of wonder, star of night,
   star with royal beauty bright,
   westward leading, still proceeding,
   guide us to thy perfect light.

2. Born a King on Bethlehem plain,
   gold I bring, to crown him again,
   King for ever, ceasing never,
   over us all to reign.

3. Frankincense to offer have I,
   Incense owns a Deity nigh.
   Prayer and praising, all men raising,
   worship him, God most high.

4. Myrrh is mine, its bitter perfume
   breathes a life of gathering gloom;
   sorrowing, sighing, bleeding, dying,
   sealed in the stone-cold tomb.

5. Glorious now behold him arise,
   King and God and sacrifice;
   alleluia, alleluia,
   earth to heaven replies.

John Henry Hopkins (1822-1900)

350

1. We will walk through the valley
   in the shadow of death.
   We will walk through the darkness
   without fear.
   Though the night may be long,
   the dark enclosing,
   we know Jesus,
   our morning light is near.

2. He has walked through the valley
   of the shadow of death,
   he has walked through the night of
   fear alone.
   Though the darkness had gathered
   to destroy him
   he was there at
   the rising of the sun.

3. We will walk in the glory
   of the bright morning sun,
   we will walk in the light that
   guides our way.
   For with Jesus the lord of
   light beside us
   we will walk in
   the glory of the day.

Michael Cockett

351

1. What can we offer you,
   Lord our God?
   How can we worship you
   as you deserve?
   We can only offer
   what our lips do proclaim.
   We can only offer you
   humble acts of praise.
   But we offer this with Jesus
   our brother, Jesus your Son.
   We join with him,
   glory to you, O God!
   We join with him,
   glory to you, O God!

2. What can we offer you,
   Lord our God?
   How can we thank you
   for all that you've done?
   We can only say it,
   Lord God, we thank you so.
   We can only try to live
   grateful lives, O Lord.
   But we offer this with Jesus,
   our brother, Jesus your Son.
   We join with him,
   our thanks to you, O God.
   We join with him,
   our thanks to you, O God.

3. What can we offer you,
   Lord our God?
   How do we prove we are
   truly sorry, Lord?
   We can say it often,
   God, sorry that we are.
   We can try to prove it,
   Lord, by the way we live.
   And we offer this with Jesus,
   our brother, Jesus, your Son.
   We join with him,
   forgive our sins, O God.
   We join with him,
   forgive our sins, O God.

4. What can we offer you,
   Lord our God?
   Dare we present you with
   another call for help?
   We just have to say it,
   Lord God, we need you so.
   We just have to beg you,
   Lord, take us by the hand.
   And we offer this with Jesus,
   our brother, Jesus, your Son.
   We join with him,
   Lord, we need you so.
   We join with him,
   Lord, we need you so.

Tom Shelley

352

Whatsoever you do
to the least of my brothers,
that you do unto me.

1. When I was hungry
   you gave me to eat.
   When I was thirsty
   you gave me to drink.
   Now enter into the
   home of my Father.

2. When I was homeless
   you opened your door.
   When I was naked
   you gave me your coat.
   Now enter into the
   home of my Father.

3. When I was weary
   you helped me find rest.
   When I was anxious
   you calmed all my fears.
   Now enter into the
   home of my Father.

4. When in a prison
   you came to my cell.
   When on a sick bed
   you cared for my needs.
   Now enter into the
   home of my Father.

5. Hurt in a battle
you bound up my wounds.
Searching for kindness
you held out your hands.
Now enter into the
home of my Father.

6. When I was Negro
or Chinese or White,
mocked and insulted,
you carried my cross.
Now enter into the
home of my Father.

7. When I was aged
you bothered to smile.
When I was restless
you listened and cared.
Now enter into the
home of my Father.

8. When I was laughed at
you stood by my side.
When I was happy
you shared in my joy.
Now enter into the
home of my Father.

W. F. Jabusch

353

1. When I needed a neighbour
    were you there were you there?
   When I needed a neighbour
    were you there?
   And the creed and the colour
    and the name won't matter
    were you there?

2. I was hungry and thirsty, . . .

3. I was cold, I was naked, . . .

4. When I needed a shelter, . . .

5. When I needed a healer, . . .

6. Wherever you travel,
    I'll be there I'll be there.
   Wherever you travel, I'll be there.
   And the creed and the colour
    and the name won't matter,
    I'll be there.

Sydney Carter

354

1. When Israel was in Egypt's land,
    let my people go,
    oppressed so hard they could not
                        stand,
    let my people go.

   Go down, Moses,
   way down in Egypt's land.
   Tell old Pharoah
   to let my people go.

2. The Lord told Moses what to do,
    let my people go,
    to lead the children of Israel
                        through,
    let my people go.

3. Your foes shall not before you stand,
    let my people go,
    and you'll possess fair Canaan's land,
    let my people go.

4. O let us all from bondage flee,
    let my people go,
    and let us all in Christ be free,
    let my people go.

5. I do believe without a doubt,
    let my people go,
    a Christian has a right to shout,
    let my people go.

Negro Spiritual

355

1. When I survey the wondrous cross
    on which the Prince of Glory died,
    my richest gain I count but loss,
    and pour contempt on all my pride.

2. Forbid it, Lord, that I should boast,
    save in the death of Christ, my God:
    all the vain things that charm me
                        most,
    I sacrifice them to his blood.

3. See from his head, his hands, his
                                 feet,
   sorrow and love flow mingled down:
   did e'er such love and sorrow meet,
   or thorns compose so rich a crown?

4. Were the whole realm of nature
                                 mine,
   that were an offering far too small;
   love so amazing, so divine,
   demands my soul, my life, my all.

Isaac Watts (1674-1748)

356

Where are you bound, Mary, Mary?
Where are you bound,
Mother of God?

1. Beauty is a dove
   sitting on a sunlit bough,
   beauty is a pray'r
   without the need of words.
   Words are more than sounds
   falling off an empty tongue:
   Let it be according to his word.

2. Mary heard the word
   spoken in her inmost heart;
   Mary bore the Word
   and held him in her arms.
   Sorrow she has known,
   seeing him upon the cross
   – greater joy to see him rise again.

3. Where are we all bound,
   carrying the Word of God?
   Time and place are ours
   to make his glory known.
   Mary bore him first,
   we will tell the whole wide world:
   Let it be according to his word.

John Glynn

357

1. Where does the wind come from?
   Where is it going?
   You see the swaying tree,
   and all the grasses blowing.

You know the wind is there,
but where?
There is no knowing.

2. Whence does the Spirit come?
   Where is his dwelling?
   You see the weary world
   so wilful, so rebelling.
   But still the Spirit breathes,
   and where,
   there is no telling.

Sister Mary Oswin

358

1. Where is love and loving-kindness,
      God is fain to dwell.
   Flock of Christ, who loved us,
      in one fold contained,
   joy and mirth be ours, for mirth
      and joy he giveth,
   fear we still and love the God who
      ever liveth,
   each to other joined by charity
      unfeignèd.

2. Where is love and loving-kindness,
      God is fain to dwell.
   Therefore, when we meet, the
      flock of Christ, so loving,
   take we heed lest bitterness be
      there engendered;
   all our spiteful thoughts and
      quarrels be surrendered,
   seeing Christ is there, divine
      among us moving.

3. Where is love and loving-kindness,
      God is fain to dwell.
   So may we be gathered once
      again, beholding
   glorified the glory, Christ, of
      thy unveiling,
   there, where never ending joy,
      and never failing
   age succeeds to age eternally
      unfolding.

From the Office of the Mandatum,
tr. R. A. Knox

359

1. Where would we be
   without Christ our Lord?
   We would be lost
   and walking in darkness
   He is the lantern
   that lights up that darkness
   and he is the shepherd
   who finds the right path.

   So let the trumpet sound to the
   *   glory of God.*
   He is our Lord, loving and wise.

2. Where would we be
   without Christ our Lord?
   We would be left
   to wander the desert.
   He is the beacon
   that leads us to safety,
   and he is the water
   that brings us new life.

3. Where would we be
   without Christ our Lord?
   We would be cold
   and starving and thirsty.
   He is the bread
   that is food for the spirit,
   and he is the wine of
   the new covenant.

4. Where would we be
   without Christ our Lord?
   He is the Son
   who saves all the nations.
   Through Christ the Son
   we are given the Spirit,
   and this is the Spirit
   who brings us new life.

   Michael Cockett

360

1. While shepherds watched
   their flocks by night,
   all seated on the ground,
   the Angel of the Lord came down,
   and glory shone around.

2. "Fear not," said he,
   (for mighty dread
   had seized their troubled mind)
   "Glad tidings of great joy I bring
   to you and all mankind.

3. "To you in David's
   town this day
   is born of David's line
   a Saviour, who is Christ the Lord;
   and this shall be the sign:

4. "The heavenly Babe
   you there shall find
   to human view displayed,
   all meanly wrapped in swathing
                            bands,
   and in a manger laid."

5. Thus spake the Seraph;
   and forthwith
   appeared a shining throng
   of Angels praising God, who thus
   addressed their joyful song:

6. "All glory be
   to God on high,
   and on the earth be peace,
   goodwill henceforth from heaven
                            to men
   begin and never cease".

   Nahum Tate (1652-1715)

361

With a song in our hearts
we shall go on our way,
to bring God's love to ev'ryone
we meet today.

Love, love, love is his name.
Love, love, love is his name.
Great, great, great is his name.
Great, great, great is his name.

With a . . .

Estelle White

362

Yahweh,
you are my strength and salvation.
Yahweh,
you are my rock and my shield.

1. When foes inside my soul
   assailed me,
   he heard my cry for help
   and came to my aid.

2. He bent the heav'ns and came
   in thunder.
   He flew to me and soared
   on wings of the wind.

3. The depths within my mind
   he showed me,
   the hidden thoughts that I
   did not know were there.

4. His arm stretched from on high
   and held me.
   He drew me from the deep,
   wild waters of self.

5. He is the lamp who lights
   the darkness.
   He guides me as I leap
   the ramparts of life.

6. I raise my voice and sing
   his glory.
   With all my heart I praise
   the God of my joy.

Estelle White

363

1. Ye choirs of new Jerusalem,
   your sweetest notes employ,
   the Paschal victory to hymn
   in strains of holy joy.

2. How Judah's Lion burst his chains,
   and crushed the serpent's head;
   and brought with him, from death's
                              domain,
   the long-imprisoned dead.

3. From hell's devouring jaws the prey
   alone our leader bore;
   his ransomed hosts pursue their way
   where he hath gone before.

4. Triumphant in his glory now
   his sceptre ruleth all:
   earth, heaven, and hell before him
                              bow
   and at his footstool fall.

5. While joyful thus his praise we sing,
   his mercy we implore,
   into his palace bright to bring,
   and keep us evermore.

6. All glory to the Father be,
   all glory to the Son,
   all glory, Holy Ghost, to thee,
   while endless ages run.

St. Fulbert of Chartres (c.1000),
tr. R. Campbell

364

1. Ye sons and daughters of the Lord!
   the king of glory, king adored,
   this day himself from death restored

   Alleluia!

2. All in the early
      morning grey
   went holy women
      on their way
   to see the tomb where Jesus lay.

3. Of spices pure
      a precious store
   in their pure hands
      those women bore,
   to anoint the sacred body o'er.

4. Then straightaway one
   in white they see,
   who saith, "Ye seek
   the Lord; but he
   is risen, and gone to Galilee".

5. This told they Peter,
   told they John;
   who forthwith to
   to the tomb are gone,
   but Peter is by John outrun.

6. That self-same night,
   while out of fear
   the doors were shut,
   their Lord most dear
   to his apostles did appear.

7. But Thomas, when
   of this he heard,
   was doubtful of
   his brethren's word;
   wherefore again
   there comes the Lord.

8. "Thomas, behold my side,"
   saith he;
   "My hands, my feet,
   my body see,
   and doubt not, but believe in me".

9. When Thomas saw
   that wounded side,
   the truth no longer
   he denied;
   "Thou art my Lord
   and God!" he cried.

10. Now let us praise
    the Lord most high,
    and strive his name
    to magnify
    on this great day,
    through earth and sky.

11. Whose mercy ever
    runneth o'er,
    whom men and angel
    hosts adore;
    to him be glory evermore.

17th c., tr. E. Caswall

365

1. Ye who own the faith of Jesus
   sing the wonders that were done,
   when the love of God the Father
   o'er our sin the victory won,
   when he made the Virgin Mary
   Mother of his only Son.

   Hail, Mary, full of grace.

2. Blessed were the chosen people
   out of whom the Lord did come,
   blessèd was the land of promise
   fashioned for his earthly home;
   but more blessèd far the mother
   she who bore him in her womb.

3. Wherefore let all faithful people
   tell the honour of her name,
   let the Church in her foreshadowed
   part in her thanksgiving claim;
   what Christ's mother sang in
   gladness
   let Christ's people sing the same

4. May the Mother's intercessions
   on our homes a blessing win,
   that the children all be prospered
   strong and fair and pure within,
   following our Lord's own footsteps,
   firm in faith and free from sin.

5. For the sick and for the aged,
   for our dear ones far away,
   for the hearts that mourn in secret,
   all who need our prayers today,
   for the faithful gone before us,
   may the holy Virgin pray.

6. Praise, O Mary, praise the Father,
   praise thy Saviour and thy Son,
   praise the everlasting Spirit,
   who hath made thee ark and throne.
   O'er all creatures high exalted,
   lowly praise the three in one.

V. S. S. Coles (1845-1929)

366 AMERICAN EUCHARIST

Lord, have mercy

Lord, have mercy.
Lord, have mercy,
on your servants, Lord, have mercy.
God Almighty, just and faithful,
Lord have mercy.
Lord, have mercy.

Christ, have mercy.
Christ, have mercy,
gift from heaven, Christ have mercy.
Light of truth, and light of justice,
Christ, have mercy.
Christ have mercy.

Lord, have mercy.
Lord, have mercy,
on your servants, Lord, have mercy.
God almighty, just and faithful,
Lord, have mercy.
Lord, have mercy.

Holy, holy, holy

Holy, holy, holy, holy,
Lord of hosts. You fill with glory
all the earth and all the heavens.
Sing hosanna, sing hosanna.

Blest and holy, blest and holy
he who comes now in the Lord's
name.
In the highest sing hosanna,
in the highest sing hosanna.

Lamb of God

Jesus, Lamb of God, have mercy,
bearer of our sins, have mercy.
Jesus, Lamb of God, have mercy,
bearer of our sins, have mercy.

Saviour of the world, Lord Jesus,
may your peace be with us always.
Saviour of the world, Lord Jesus,
may your peace be with us always.

Sandra Joan Billington

367 ISRAELI MASS

Lord, have mercy

Lord, have mercy.
Lord, have mercy.
Lord, have mercy on us all.
Lord, have mercy.
Lord, have mercy
Lord, have mercy on us all.

Christ, have mercy.
Christ, have mercy.
Christ, have mercy on us all.
Christ, have mercy.
Christ, have mercy.
Christ, have mercy on us all.

Lord, have mercy.
Lord, have mercy.
Lord, have mercy on us all.
Lord, have mercy.
Lord, have mercy.
Lord, have mercy on us all.

Holy, holy, holy

Holy, holy, holy, holy
Lord of power, Lord of might.
Heav'n and earth are filled with
glory.
Sing hosanna evermore.

Blest and holy, blest and holy
he who comes from God on high.
Raise your voices, sing his glory,
praise his name for evermore.

Lamb of God

Lamb of God,
you take away the sin,
the sin of all the world.
Give us mercy,
give us mercy,
give us mercy, Lamb of God.

Lamb of God,   *(Repeat)*
you take away the sin,
the sin of all the world.
Grant us peace, Lord,
grant us peace, Lord,
grant us peace, O Lamb of God.

Anthony Hamson

368 GEORDIE MASS

Lord have mercy
Lord, have mercy on us all.
Lord, have mercy on us.
Lord, have mercy on us all.
Lord, have mercy on us.

Christ, have mercy on us all.
Christ, have mercy on us.
Christ, have mercy on us all.
Christ, have mercy on us.

Lord, have mercy on us all.
Lord, have mercy on us.
Lord, have mercy on us all.
Lord, have mercy on us.

Holy, holy, holy
Holy, holy, holy Lord
God of might and God of pow'r.
Glory fills all heav'n and earth.
Sing to him hosanna!

Blessed is the one who comes
in the name of Christ our Lord.
Holy, holy, holy Lord.
Sing to him hosanna!

Lamb of God
Lamb of God, you take our sins,
take away our sins, Lord.
So have mercy on us all,
so have mercy on us.   *(Repeat)*

Lamb of God, you take our sins,
take away our sins, Lord.
Grant us peace, O grant us peace,
grant us peace for ever.

Anthony Hamson

369 MONMOUTHSHIRE MASS

Lord, have mercy
Lord, have mercy on us all.
Lord, have mercy on us.
Lord, have mercy on us all.
Lord, have mercy on us.

Christ, have mercy on us all.
Christ have mercy on us.
Christ, have mercy on us all
Christ have mercy on us.

Lord, have mercy on us all.
Lord, have mercy on us.
Lord, have mercy on us all.
Lord, have mercy on us.

Holy, holy, holy
Holy, holy, holy Lord,
God of might and power.
Glory fills all heav'n and earth.
Sing to him hosanna!

Blessed is the one who comes
bringing this great glory.
Praise and honour be to God.
Sing to him hosanna!

Lamb of God
Lamb of God, you take away
the sin of all the world.
Lamb of God, you take away
the sin of all the world.

Lamb of God, you take away
the sin of all the world.
Grant us peace, O Lamb of God,
grant us peace for ever.

Anthony Hamson

370 SWEDISH MASS

Lord, have mercy
Lord, have mercy on us all.
Lord, have mercy on us.
Lord, have mercy on us all.
Lord, have mercy on us.

Christ, have mercy on us all.
Christ, have mercy on us.
Christ, have mercy on us all.
Christ, have mercy on us.

Lord, have mercy on us all.
Lord, have mercy on us.
Lord, have mercy on us all.
Lord, have mercy on us.

Holy, holy, holy

Holy, holy, holy Lord,
earth is full of your glory.
Glory fills the heavens too.
Sing to him hosanna!

Blessed is the one who comes
bringing this great glory.
Holy, holy, holy Lord.
Sing to him hosanna!

Lamb of God
Lamb of God, O Jesus Christ,
take away our sins,
and have mercy on us all,
and have mercy on us.   *(Repeat)*
Lamb of God, O Jesus Christ,
take away our sins.
Grant us peace, O grant us peace,
grant us peace for ever.

Anthony Hamson

371 PILGRIM'S MASS

Lord have mercy
1. Lord, have mercy on my soul.
   Lord, have mercy on my soul.
   Lord, have mercy, Lord have mercy,
   Lord, have mercy on my soul.

2. Christ, have mercy on my soul,
   Christ have mercy on my soul.
   Christ, have mercy, Christ have
   mercy,
   Christ, have mercy on my soul.

3. Pray for me, pray for me,
   brothers and sisters, pray for me.
   Lord, have mercy on my soul.
   Lord, have mercy on my soul.

4. I confess that I have sinned,
   sinned in thought and word and
   deed,
   done the things I should not do,
   left undone what I should do.

Repeat Verse 1

Gloria

1. Glory be to God in heaven,
   glory be to God on high,
   glory be, we give you thanks
   for the glory of the universe.

2. Peace on earth to all creation,
   peace on earth to all God's friends,

peace on earth to everyone
through the mercy of our Lord
Jesus Christ.

3. Jesus Christ, the Son of the Father,
   Jesus Christ, the Son of Man,
   Jesus Christ, the Lamb of God
   who takes away the sins of the
   world.

4. Lamb of God, right hand of the
   Father,
   Lamb of God the sacrifice,
   Lamb of God who bore our sins,
   have mercy on us, receive our pray'r.

5. You alone are the Lord of creation,
   you alone are the Holy One,
   you alone are the three in one,
   the Father, the Son and the Spirit.

6. Glory be, glory be,
   glory be, glory be.   Amen.

Creed

1. I believe.
   I believe that God almighty
   made the world for us to use.
   I believe in good and evil
   and that we've the power to choose.

2. I believe.
   I believe in God the Father.
   I believe in God the Son.
   I believe that he was born
   on earth to save us every one.

3. I believe.
   I believe he loved and suffered,
   taught us how to live and die,
   showed us all the way to heaven
   in our hearts, not in the sky.

4. I believe.
   I believe that God the Spirit
   ever was since time began.
   I believe that he will judge our
   actions when we've lived our span.

5. I believe.
   I believe the church is holy,
   I believe the church is true.
   I believe the church was made for
   all men, not just me and you.

6. I believe.
   Doubts and fears will fall upon us;
   we must trust that God will guide.
   Faith and hope and love will help us,
   and in joy we will abide.

Sanctus

Holy, holy, holy Lord God of hosts.
Your glory fills all heaven and earth.
Hosanna in the highest.
Holy, holy, holy Lord God of hosts.
Blessed is he who comes in your name.
Hosanna in the highest.

Lord's Prayer

Our Father, king of heav'n and earth
we praise thy sacred name.

1. Thy kingdom come, thy will be done
   in thought and deed not in words
                                    alone.

2. Give us this day our daily bread,
   our spirits and our bodies fed.

3. And forgive us all our trespasses,
   while we in turn will do no less.

4. And keep us from temptation's way,
   and help us when we go astray.

Lamb of God
Lamb of God,
you take away the sins of the world,
have mercy on us.
Lamb of God,
you take away the sins of the world,
have mercy on us.
Lamb of God,
you take away the sins of the world,
have mercy on us, and grant us peace.

Gordon Rock

372

1. O salutaris hostia,
   Quae caeli pandis ostium,
   Bella premunt hostilia,
   Da robur, fer auxilium.

2. Uni trinoque Domino
   Sit sempiterna gloria,
   Qui vitam sine termino
   Nobis donet in patria. Amen.

373
English version

1. O saving victim, opening wide
   The gate of heav'n to man below;
   Our foes press on from ev'ry side;
   Thine aid supply, thy strength bestow.

2. To thy great name be endless praise,
   Immortal Godhead, one in three;
   O grant us endless length of days
   In our true native land with thee.
                                    Amen.

St. Thomas Aquinas (1227-74),
tr. J.M. Neale, E. Caswall and others

374

1. Tantum ergo Sacramentum
   Veneremur cernui:
   Et antiquum documentum
   Novo cedat ritui;
   Praestet fides supplementum
   Sensuum defectui.

2. Genitori, genitoque
   Laus et jubiliatio,
   Salus, honor, virtus quoque
   Sit et benedictio;
   Procedenti ab utroque
   Compar sit laudatio. Amen.

375

English version

1. Therefore we, before him bending,
   This great sacrament revere;
   Types and shadows have their ending,
   For the newer rite is here;
   Faith, our outward sense befriending,
   Makes the inward vision clear.

2. Glory let us give, and blessing
   To the Father and the Son,
   Honour, might, and praise addressing,
   While eternal ages run;
   Ever too his love confessing
   Who from both, with both is one.
                                    Amen.

St. Thomas Aquinas (1227-74),
tr. J.M. Neale, E. Caswall and others

Index of First Lines

Abide with me	1	Colours of day	45
Accept, O Father, in thy love	2	Come, adore this wondrous presence	46
All creation, bless the Lord	3		
All creatures of our God and King	4	Come, Christian people	47
Alleluia	5	Come, come, come to the manger	48
Alleluia, I will praise the Father	6	Come down, O love divine	49
Alleluia, sing to Jesus	7	Come, Holy Ghost, Creator, come	50
All glory, laud and honour	8	Come, Lord Jesus, come	51
All hail the power of Jesus' name	9	Come, my brothers	52
All people that on earth do dwell	10	Come, praise the Lord	53
All that I am	11	Come to the Lord	54
All the nations of the earth	12	Come, ye thankful people, come	55
All things bright and beautiful	13	Crown him with many crowns	56
All this world belongs to Jesus	14	Daily, daily sing to Mary	57
All ye who seek a comfort sure	15	Day by day in the market place	58
All you peoples, clap your hands	16	Day is done, but love unfailing	59
Almighty Father, Lord most high	17	Dear Lord and Father of mankind	60
Almighty Father, take this bread	18	Dear maker of the starry skies	61
Amazing Grace	19	Ding! dong! merrily on high	62
And did those feet in ancient time	20	Do not worry	63
Angels we have heard in heaven	21	Do you know that the Lord	64
Angels we have heard on high	22	Draw nigh, and take the body	65
Ask and you will receive	23	Dust, dust and ashes	66
As with gladness men of old	24	Eternal Father, strong to save	67
Attend and keep this happy fast	25	Faith of our fathers	68
At the cross her station keeping	26	Father and life-giver	69
At the Lamb's high feast we sing	27	Father most holy	70
At the name of Jesus	28	Father, within thy house today	71
Ave Maria, O maiden, O mother	29	Feed us now	72
Away in a manger	30	Fight the good fight	73
Battle is o'er, hell's armies flee	31	Fill my house unto the fullest	74
Be still and know I am with you	32	Firmly I believe and truly	75
Be still and know that I am God	33	Follow Christ	76
Bethlehem of noblest cities	34	For all the saints	77
Be thou my vision, O Lord of my heart	35	Forth in the peace of Christ we go	78
		Forth in thy name O Lord, I go	79
Blest are the pure in heart	36	Forty days and forty nights	80
Breathe on me breath of God	37	From the deep I lift my voice	81
Bring, all ye dear-bought nations bring	38	From the depths we cry to thee	82
		Give me peace, O Lord, I pray	83
Bring flowers of the rarest	39	Give me joy in my heart	84
By the blood that flowed	40	Give me yourself	85
Christ be beside me	41	Glorious God, King of Creation	86
Christ is king of earth and heaven	42	Glory be to God the King	87
Christ is our King	43	Glory be to Jesus	88
Christ the Lord is risen today	44	Glory to God (Peruvian Gloria)	89

Glory to thee, Lord God	90	Into one we all are gathered	139
Glory to thee, my God, this night	91	I saw the grass	140
Go tell it on the mountain	92	I sing a song to you, Lord	141
God be in my head	93	I sing the Lord God's praises	142
God everlasting	94	It came upon a midnight clear	143
Godhead here in hiding	95	It's me, O Lord	144
God is love	96	I will give you glory	146
God is love: his the care	97	I wonder as I wander	147
God of mercy and compassion	98	January brings the snow	148
God's spirit is in my heart	99	Jerusalem the golden	149
Going home	100	Jesu, lover of my soul	150
Gonna lay down my sword	101	Jesu, meek and lowly	151
Go, the Mass is ended	102	Jesu, the very thought of thee	152
Great St. Andrew, friend of Jesus	103	Jesus Christ is risen today	153
Guide me, O thou great Redeemer	104	Jesus, gentlest Saviour	154
Hail, glorious St. Patrick	105	Jesus, Lord, I'll sing a song	155
Hail, Queen of heaven	106	Jesus is God! the solid earth	156
Hail Redeemer, King divine	107	Jesus, my Lord, my God, my all	157
Hail, the day that sees him rise	108	Jesus, thou art coming	158
Hail, thou star of ocean	109	Just a closer walk with thee	159
Hail to the Lord's anointed	110	Keep we the fast that men of old	160
Happy the man	111	King of glory, king of peace	161
Hark! a herald voice is calling	112	Kum ba yah	162
Hark! the herald angels sing	113	Leader now on earth no longer	163
Haul away	114	Lead, kindly light	164
Help, Lord, the souls	115	Lead us, heavenly Father, lead us	165
Here's a child for you, O Lord	116	Let all mortal flesh keep silence	166
He's got the whole world	117	Let all that is within me	167
He was born like you and I	118	Let all the world	168
He who would valiant be	119	Let us break bread together	169
Holy Father, God of might	120	Let's make peace in our hearts	170
Holy God we praise thy name	121	Let us with a gladsome mind	171
Holy, holy, holy Lord	122	Light of our darkness	172
Holy, holy, holy Lord God	123	Little flower in the ground	173
Holy Spirit, Lord of light	124	Little Jesus sweetly sleep	174
Holy Spirit of fire	125	Long ago in Bethlehem	175
Holy Virgin, by God's decree	126	Look down, O Mother Mary	176
How dark was the stable	127	Lord, accept the gifts we offer	177
I am the bread of life	128	Lord for tomorrow and its needs	178
I believe in God almighty	129	Lord, Jesus Christ	179
I believe in God, the Father	130	Lord Jesus, think on me	180
I danced in the morning	131	Lord of all hopefulness	181
I'll sing a hymn to Mary	132	Lord, we pray for golden peace	182
Immaculate Mary	133	Lord, who throughout these forty	
Immortal, invisible, God only wise	134	days	183
In bread we bring you, Lord	135	Love divine, all loves excelling	184
In Christ there is no east or west	136	Love is his word, love is his way	185
In the bleak mid-winter	137	Loving Father, from thy bounty	186
In the earth the small seed	138	Loving shepherd of thy sheep	187

Maiden, yet a mother	188	O my Lord, within my heart	237
Make me a channel of your peace	189	Once in royal David's city	238
Man of Galilee	190	On Jordan's bank the Baptist's cry	239
Many times I have turned	191	On this house your blessing, Lord	240
Mary immaculate	192	Onward Christian soldiers	241
May the peace of Christ	193	Open your ears	242
Merrily on	194	O perfect love	243
Mine eyes have seen the glory	195	O praise ye the Lord	244
Morning has broken	196	O Priest and Victim, Lord of life	245
Moses I know you're the man	197	O purest of creatures	246
Most ancient of all mysteries	198	O sacred head sore wounded	247
Mother of mercy, day by day	199	O sacred heart	248
My glory and the lifter	200	O thou, who at thy Eucharist	249
My God, accept my heart this day	201	O Trinity, most blessed light	250
My God, and is thy table spread	202	Our Father (Caribbean)	251
My God, how wonderful thou art	203	Out and away	252
My God, I love thee, not because	204	O worship the king	253
My God loves me	205	Peace is flowing like a river	254
My song is love unknown	206	Peace is the gift of heaven	255
New praises be given	207	Peacemakers	256
Now come to me all you who seek	208	Peace, perfect peace	257
Now Jesus said.	209	People of God, give praise	258
Now Jesus said: You must love	210	Praise him, praise him	259
Now thank we all our God	211	Praise my soul, the king of heaven	260
Now with the fast-departing light	212	Praise the Lord	261
O bread of heaven	213	Praise to the holiest	262
O come, all ye faithful	214	Praise to the Lord our God	263
O come and mourn with me	215	Praise to the Lord, the almighty	264
O come, O come Emmanuel	216	Praise we now the Lord our God	265
O Father, now the hour has come	217	Praise we our God with joy	266
O Father, take in sign of love	218	Promised Lord and Christ is he	267
Of the Glorious Body telling	219	Reap me the earth	268
O Godhead hid,	220	Rejoice in the Lord	269
O God of earth and altar	221	Rejoice! the Lord is King	270
O God, our help in ages past	222	Ride on, ride on in majesty	271
O God, thy people gather	223	Round me falls the night	272
O God, we give ourselves today	224	Seasons come, seasons go	273
Oh living water	225	See amid the winter's snow	274
Oh Lord, all the world	226	See us, Lord, about thine altar	275
Oh Lord, my God	227	Shalom	276
O Holy Lord, by all adored	228	Silent night	277
Oh, sinner man	229	Sing, my soul	278
Oh, the Lord looked down	230	Sing, my tongue	279
Oh the love of my Lord	231	Sing of the bride	280
Oh, when the Saints	232	Sing of Mary, pure and lowly	281
O Jesus Christ, remember	233	Sing, people of God	282
O King of might and splendour	234	Sing praises to God	283
O little town of Bethlehem	235	Sing praises to the living God	284
O mother blest	236	Sleep, holy babe	285

Songs of thankfulness and praise	286	To the name that brings salvation	335
Sons of God	287	Trust in the eyes of a tiny babe	336
Soul of my Saviour	288	Unto us is born a Son	337
Spirit of the living God	289	Vaster far than any ocean	338
Star of ocean, lead us	290	Virgin wholly marvellous	339
Steal away to Jesus	291	Walk with me, oh my Lord	340
Suffer little children	292	We are gathering together	341
Sweet heart of Jesus	293	We are one in the Spirit	342
Sweet Sacrament divine	294	We bring our gifts to the Lord	343
Sweet Saviour bless us 'ere we go	295	We celebrate this festive day	344
Take my hands	296	We gather together	345
Take our bread, we ask you	297	We plough the fields and scatter	346
Thank you	298	Were you there?	347
The bakerwoman	299	We shall overcome	348
The Church's one foundation	300	We three kings of Orient are	349
The coming of our God	301	We will walk through the valley	350
The day of resurrection	302	What can we offer you?	351
The day thou gavest, Lord	303	Whatsoever you do	352
The farmer in the fertile field	304	When I needed a neighbour	353
The first Nowell	305	When Israel was in Egypt's land	354
The God whom earth and sea	306	When I survey the wondrous cross	355
The green life rises from the earth	307	Where are you bound, Mary	356
The head that once was crowned	308	Where does the wind	357
The heavenly word,	309	Where is love and loving kindness	358
The King of Glory comes	310	Where would we be without Christ	359
The King of Love my shepherd is	311	While shepherds watched	360
The Lord's my shepherd	312	With a song in our hearts	361
The Mass is ended	313	Yahweh, you are my strength	362
The prophet in his hunger	314	Ye choirs of new Jerusalem	363
The race that long in darkness	315	Ye sons and daughters of the Lord	364
There is a green hill	316	Ye who own the faith of Jesus	365
There is a world	317		
The royal banners forward go	318		
The Spirit of the Lord	319	*Mass Settings*	
The tree of life	320	Geordie Mass	368
The Virgin Mary had a baby boy	321	American Eucharist	366
The wandering flock of Israel	322	Swedish Mass	370
They hung him on a cross	323	Monmouthshire Mass	369
They say I am wise	324	Israeli Mass	367
This day God give me	325	Pilgrim's Mass	371
This is the image of the Queen	326		
This is my will	327		
This joyful Eastertide	328	*Benediction*	
This little light of mine	329	O Salutaris	372
Thou wilt keep him	330	O saving victim	373
Thy hand, O God, has guided	331	Therefore, we before him bending	375
To Christ the Lord of worlds	332	Tantum Ergo	374
To Christ the Prince of peace	333		
To Jesus' heart all burning	334		

Index of Uses

THE MASS

ENTRANCE
Alleluia	5
Come my brothers	52
Come to the Lord	54
Fill my house	74
It's me, O Lord	144
Let all mortal flesh keep silence	166
My God and is thy table spread	202
Open your ears	242
People of God give praise	258
Praise him	259
Rejoice in the Lord	269
See us Lord about thine altar	275
Sing praises to God	283
The green life rises from the earth	307
We celebrate this festive day	344
We gather together	345

GOSPEL ACCLAMATION
Alleluia	5
Rejoice the Lord	270
Spirit of the living God	289
The Spirit of the Lord	319

CREED
I believe in God almighty	129

See also under 'Pilgrim's Mass'

OFFERTORY
Accept O Father	2
All that I am	11
Almighty Father Lord most high	17
Almighty Father take this bread	18
Come Lord Jesus	51
Father and life giver	69
Fill my house	74
Glory to thee, my God, this night	91
Holy, Holy, Holy	123
In bread we bring you Lord,	135
Let us break bread together	169
Lord accept the gifts we offer	177
My God loves me	205
O God, we give ourselves today	224
O king of might and splendour	234
People of God give praise	258
Reap me the earth	268
Take my hands	296
Take our bread we ask you	297
We are gathering together	341
We bring our gifts	343
What can we offer you?	351

GREAT AMEN
A setting is given in the organ edition.

OUR FATHER
Our Father (Caribbean)	251

The music for Estelle White's setting is given in the organ edition. No words are given in the edition since they are known by everyone. See also under 'Pilgrim's Mass'

SIGN OF PEACE
Give me peace, O Lord	83
Gonna lay down my sword and shield	101
May the peace of Christ be with you today	193
Peace is the gift of heaven	255
Peace, perfect peace	257

COMMUNION
Alleluia, sing to Jesus	7
Come, Lord Jesus, come	51
Draw nigh and take the body	65
Fill my house	74
Give me yourself	85
Godhead here in hiding	95
I am the bread of life	128
In Christ there is no east or west	136
Into one we are all gathered	139
In the earth the small seed	138
I saw the grass	140
I watch the sunrise	145
Jesus, thou art coming	158
Let all that is within me	167
Let us break bread together on our knees	169
Let's make peace	170

Love is his word   185
Now Jesus said   209
O bread of heaven,   213
Oh Lord, all the World   226
Oh the love of my Lord   231
Peace is the gift of heaven   255
Peace perfect peace   257
The green life rises from the earth   307
The prophet in his hunger   314
This is my will   327
We gather together   345
Where is love and loving kindness   358

RECESSIONAL
Colours of day   45
Glory to thee, Lord God   90
God's spirit is in my heart   99
Go, the Mass is ended   102
O thou who at thy Eucharist   249
Peace, perfect peace   257
Praise him   259
Shalom   276
The Mass is ended   313
Walk with me, Oh my Lord   340
With a song in our hearts   361

MASS SETTINGS
American Eucharist   366
Geordie Mass   368
Israeli Mass   367
Monmouthshire Mass   369
Swedish Mass   370
Pilgrim's Mass   371

BENEDICTION
O salutaris — O saving Victim   372
Tantum Ergo — Therefore we
     before him   374

THE SACRAMENTS

BAPTISM
Colours of day   45
Come down, O love divine   49
Come, Holy Ghost, Creator, come   50
Firmly I believe and truly   75
Here's a child for you, O Lord   116
Immortal, invisible, God only wise   134
Love is his word, love is his way   185

Oh living water   225

PENANCE
Forty days and forty nights   80
From the deep I lift my voice   81
God of mercy and compassion   98
It's me O Lord   144
Many times I have turned   199
My glory and the lifter of my head   200
Now come to me   208
Oh Lord my God   227
O sacred head sore wounded   247
Seasons come, seasons go   273
Thou wilt keep him in perfect
     peace   330
Walk with me   340
We will walk   350
Yahweh, you are my strength   362

CONFIRMATION
See under 'Pentecost, Confirmation,
The Holy Spirit'

MARRIAGE
Father, within thy house today   71
O perfect love   243
Sing of the bride   280
The Lord's my shepherd   312

FUNERALS
For all the saints   77
From the deep I lift my voice   81
Going Home   100
Jerusalem the golden   149
Lead, kindly light   164
Now come to me   208
Oh Lord, my God   227
Steal away   291
The Lord's my shepherd   312
We will walk through the valley   350

THE CHURCH'S YEAR
ADVENT
Hail to the Lord's anointed   110
Hark! a herald voice is calling   112
O come, O come Emmanuel   216
On Jordan's bank the Baptist's cry   239
Promised Lord and Christ is he   267
The coming of our God   301

CHRISTMAS

Angels we have heard in heaven	21
Angels we have heard on high	22
As with gladness men of old	24
Away in a manger	30
Come Christian people	47
Come, come, come to the manger	48
Ding dong merrily on high	62
Go tell it on the mountain	92
Hark! the herald angels sing	113
How dark was the stable	127
In the bleak mid-winter	137
It came upon the midnight clear	143
I wonder as I wander	147
Little Jesus, sweetly sleep	174
Long ago in Bethlehem	175
O come all ye faithful	214
O little town of Bethlehem	235
Once in Royal David's city	238
See, amid the winter's snow	274
Silent night	277
Sleep, holy babe	285
The first Nowell	305
The Virgin Mary had a baby boy	321
Unto us is born a Son	337
We three kings of Orient are	349
While shepherds watched	360

EPIPHANY

Bethlehem of noblest cities	34
Songs of thankfulness and praise	286
The race that long in darkness	315
We three kings of Orient are	349

LENT

Attend and keep this happy fast	25
At the cross her station keeping	26
Crown him with many crowns	56
Forty days and forty nights	80
From the deep I lift my voice	81
From the depths we cry to thee	82
God of mercy and compassion	98
Keep we the fast that men of old	160
Lord, who throughout these forty days	183
O come and mourn	215
O sacred head sore wounded	247

The Lord's my shepherd	312
Walk with me, oh my Lord	340
See also under 'Penance'	

HOLY WEEK

All glory, laud and honour	8
All ye who seek a comfort sure	15
By the blood that flowed from thee	40
Glory be to Jesus	88
Jesu, meek and lowly	151
O come and mourn with me awhile	215
Of the glorious Body telling	219
O sacred head sore wounded	247
Ride on, ride on in majesty	271
Sing my tongue, the glorious battle	279
The royal banners forward go	318
They hung him on a cross	323
When I survey the wondrous cross	355

EASTER

At the lamb's high feast we sing	27
Battle is o'er, hell's armies flee	31
Bring, all you dear-bought nations	38
Christ the Lord is risen today	44
Dust, dust and ashes	66
He was born like you and I	118
Jesus Christ is risen today	153
Now Jesus said	209
The bakerwoman	299
The day of resurrection	302
They hung him on a cross	323
This joyful Eastertide	328
Were you there?	347
We will walk through the valley	350
Ye choirs of New Jerusalem	363
Ye sons and daughters of the Lord	364

ASCENSION

Hail, the day that sees him rise	108
New praises be given	207

PENTECOST, CONFIRMATION, THE HOLY SPIRIT

Breathe on me breath of God	37
Colours of day	45
Come down, O love divine	49
Come Holy Ghost, Creator, come	50
God's Spirit is in my heart	99
He who would valiant be	119

Holy, holy, holy,	123	**CHRIST THE KING**	
Holy spirit Lord of light	124	Christ is our king	43
Holy Spirit of fire	125	Hail, Redeemer, King divine!	107
Love is his word, love is his way	185	King of glory, king of peace	161
Oh living water	225	Praise we now the Lord our God	265
Out and away	252	To Christ the Lord of worlds	332
Peace is the gift of heaven	255		
Spirit of the living God	289	**BLESSED VIRGIN**	
The church's one foundation	300	Ave Maria, O Maiden, O Mother	29
Thy hand O Lord has guided	331	Bring flowers of the rarest	39
Trust in the eyes of a tiny babe	336	Daily, daily sing to Mary	57
We are one in Spirit	342	Hail, Queen of heaven	106
Where does the wind come from?	357	Hail, thou star of ocean	109
		Holy Virgin, by God's decree	126
TRINITY		I'll sing a hymn to Mary	132
Eternal Father, strong to save	67	Immaculate Mary!	133
Father most holy	70	Look down, O Mother Mary	176
Holy God, we praise thy name	121	Maiden, yet a mother	188
Holy, holy, holy, Lord God	123	Mary immaculate	192
Lead us heavenly Father, lead us	165	Mother of mercy, day by day	199
Merrily on	193	O Mother blest	236
Most ancient of all mysteries	198	O purest of creatures!	246
O Trinity, most blessed light	250	Sing of Mary, pure and lowly	281
Sing praises to the living God	284	Star of ocean, lead us	290
		The bakerwoman	299
CORPUS CHRISTI		The God whom earth and sea	306
Godhead here in hiding	95	This is the image of the Queen	326
Jesus my Lord, my God, my all	157	Virgin wholly marvellous	339
O bread of heaven	213	Where are you bound, Mary?	356
Of the glorious Body telling	219	Ye who own the faith of Jesus	365
O Godhead hid	220		
O Jesus Christ, remember	233	**SAINTS**	
O Salutaris Hostia O saving victim	372	For all the saints	77
Sweet Sacrament divine	294	Great St. Andrew, friend of Jesus	103
Tantum ergo		Hail glorious Saint Patrick	105
Therefore we, before him	374	Jerusalem the golden	149
The heavenly Word, proceeding		Leader now on earth no longer	163
forth	309		
See also under 'Communion'		**MARTYRS**	
		Faith of our fathers	68
SACRED HEART			
Sweet heart of Jesus	293	**HOLY SOULS**	
To Christ the Prince of Peace	333	Help, Lord, the souls	115
To Jesus heart all burning	334		
		UNITY, THE CHURCH	
PRECIOUS BLOOD		Christ be beside me	41
Alleluia, sing to Jesus	7	Colours of day	45
Glory be to Jesus	88	Come to the Lord	54

Do you know that the Lord?	64	We gather together	345
Feed us now	72	We shall overcome	348
Follow Christ	76	When Israel was in Egypt's Land	354
God's Spirit is in my heart	99		
He's got the whole world	117	HARVEST	
In Christ there is no east or west	136	In the earth the small seed	138
Let's make peace	170	We plough the fields	346
Lord, we pray for golden peace	182		
Make me a channel of your peace	189	MORNING	
Moses, I know you're the man	197	Morning has broken	196
Open your ears	242		
Peace is the gift of heaven	255	EVENING	
Sons of God	287	I watch the sunrise	145
Thy hand, O God, has guided	331	Round me falls the night	272
We are one in the Spirit	342	Sweet Saviour bless us	295

Acknowledgements

The publishers wish to express their gratitude to the following for permission to include copyright material in this book:

A.R. Mowbray & Co. Ltd., for *This Joyful Eastertide* and *Unto us is born a Son.*

Roberton Publications (for J. Curwen & Sons Ltd.) for *All Creatures of our God and King.*

Josef Weinberger Ltd., for *All Creation, bless the Lord; O Lord, all the world belongs to you* and *Lord, Jesus Christ.*

The Literary Estate of Eleanor Hull and Chatto and Windus Ltd., for *A Prayer (Be thou my vision)* from The Poem Book of the Gael.

Rev. Willard F. Jabusch, for *All this world belongs to Jesus; Many times I have turned; The King of glory comes; We celebrate this festive day; We gather together; Whatsoever you do;* and *Open your ears.*

The Right Rev. Monsignor David McRoberts, for *Praise we now the Lord our God.*

A. Gregory Murray for *O King of might and splendour.*

Rev. Clifford Howell, S.J., for *Glory to thee, O Lord; O God thy people gather; O God we give ourselves today* and *See us, Lord, about thine altar.*

Christopher Alston for *Father, most holy.*

Shalom Community, 1504 Polk, Wichita Falls, Texas for *O living water* and *I sing a song to you, Lord.*

Belwin Mills Music Ltd for *Suffer little children.* Reproduced by kind permission of the copyright owners Belwin Mills Music Ltd, 250 Purley Way, Croydon, CR9 4QD.

Stainer & Bell Ltd. for *Lord of the dance* and *When I needed a neighbour.*

Oxford University Press for *God is love, his the care* (Songs of Praise); *He who would valiant be* (English Hymnal); *O God of earth and altar* and *O perfect love.*

Bosworth & Co. Ltd of 14/18 Heddon Street, London, W1R 8DP for *Thank you.*

Thankyou Music of 10 Seaforth Avenue, New Malden, Surrey for *Light up the fire.* © 1973.

Rev. Roger Ruston, O.P., for *Attend and keep this happy fast* and *Promised Lord and Christ is he.*

Vanguard Music for *God's spirit is in my heart; Let trumpets sound; The bakerwoman* and *Sing of the bride.*

Franciscan Communications Centre of Los Angeles for *Sing praises to the living God; Lord, we pray for golden peace; Sing, people of God; Follow Christ; All that I am; Glorious God; The Mass is ended; Leave it in the hands of the Lord; Happy the men; Make me a channel of your peace* and *Take my hands.*